The Speech. Page 93.

*f*P

Also by Chris Hedges

WAR IS A FORCE THAT GIVES US MEANING

WHAT EVERY PERSON SHOULD KNOW ABOUT WAR

LOSING MOSES

— *on the* —

FREEWAY

*The 10 Commandments
in America*

CHRIS HEDGES

FREE PRESS

NEW YORK LONDON TORONTO SYDNEY

*f*P

FREE PRESS
A Division of Simon & Schuster, Inc.
1230 Avenue of the Americas
New York, NY 10020

FREE PRESS and colophon are trademarks
of Simon & Schuster, Inc.

For information about special discounts for bulk purchases,
please contact Simon & Schuster Special Sales at
1-800-456-6798 or business@simonandschuster.com

Designed by Joseph Rutt

Manufactured in the United States of America

10   9   8   7   6   5   4   3   2   1

Library of Congress Cataloging-in-Publication Data
Hedges, Chris.
Losing Moses on the freeway : the 10 commandments in America / Chris
Hedges.
    p. cm.
Includes bibliographical references and index.
1. Ten commandments. 2. United States—Moral conditions. 3. Hedges, Chris.
I. Title.

BV4655.H374 2005
241.5′2—dc22   2005040619

ISBN 0-7432-5513-5

For Kim, whose patience, gentleness and compassion I seek every day to emulate and whose love saved me

And the people stood afar off, while Moses drew near to the thick darkness where God was.

—Exodus 20:21

CONTENTS

LOSING MOSES
— *on the* —
FREEWAY

THE 10 COMMANDMENTS

———◆—

You shall have no other gods before me.

You shall not make for yourself a graven image, or any likeness
of anything that is in heaven above, or that is in the earth
beneath, or that is in the water under the earth; you shall not
bow down to them, or serve them.

You shall not take the name of the Lord your God in vain.

Remember the sabbath day, to keep it holy.

Honor your father and your mother.

You shall not kill.

You shall not commit adultery.

You shall not steal.

You shall not bear false witness against your neighbor.

You shall not covet your neighbor's house.

PROLOGUE

The commandments are a list of religious edicts, according to passages in Exodus and Deuteronomy, given to Moses by God on Mount Sinai. The first four are designed to guide the believer toward a proper relationship with God. The remaining six deal with our relations with others. It is these final six commands that are given the negative form of "You Shall Not. . . ." Only two of the commandments, the prohibitions against stealing and murder, are incorporated into our legal code. Protestants, Catholics and Jews have compiled slightly different lists, but the core demands of the commandments remain the same. Muslims, while they do not list the commandments in the Koran, honor the laws of Moses, whom they see as a prophet.

The commandments are one of the earliest attempts to lay down rules and guidelines to sustain community. The commandments include the most severe violations and moral dilemmas in human life, although these violations often lie beyond the scope of the law. They were for the ancients, and are for us, the rules that, when honored, hold us together and when dishonored lead to alienation, discord and violence.

The commandments choose us. We are rarely able to choose them. We do not, however hard we work to insulate ourselves, ultimately control our fate. We cannot save ourselves from betrayal, theft, envy, greed, deception and murder, nor always from the impulses that propel us to commit these acts. These violations, often committed without warning, can leave deep, lifelong wounds. Most of us wrestle profoundly with at least one of these violations.

My renewed fascination with the depth and breadth of the commandments came shortly after I returned to New York City after nearly two decades as a foreign correspondent who covered conflicts in Latin America, Africa, the Middle East and the former Yugoslavia. I was unsure of where I was headed. I had lost the emotional and physical resiliency that allowed me to cope in war. I was plagued by memories I wanted to forget, waking suddenly in the middle of the night, my sleep shattered by visions of gunfire and death. I felt alienated from those around me, unaccustomed to the common language and images imposed by popular culture, unable to communicate the pain and suffering I had witnessed, not much interested in building a career.

We lived in a tiny apartment in Manhattan. My son and daughter shared a bedroom. The monthly mortgage payments plunged me into debt. I had, in the past, rarely seen or spoken with editors, who were hundreds or thousands of miles away. I was uncomfortable in the newsroom. My solace came in walking the streets of the city after taking my son and daughter to school. I started early one morning at the very bottom of Manhattan. I walked eighty blocks uptown, peering into some shops, ignoring others, brushing past the mix of races and nationalities, listening to the variety of languages and the din of the streets. These mosaics comforted me. There are too many differences in New York to force iron conformity. I had reported from over fifty countries. The narrow definitions of race, religion and nation had been broadened and erased by friendship and experience, by the recognition that those we sometimes find alien and strange often reflect back to us parts of ourselves we do not understand.

The Brooklyn Academy of Music was showing a ten-part series called The Decalogue. "The Decalogue" is the classical name of the 10 Commandments. "Deka-," in Greek, means ten. "Logos" means saying or speech. The director, I read in the announcement, was the Polish filmmaker Krzysztof Kieslowski who had made a trilogy called *White, Blue and Red.* The Decalogue films, each about an hour and based on one of the commandments, were to be shown two at a time over five consecutive weeks. I saw them on Sunday nights, taking the subway to Brooklyn, its cars rocking and screeching along the tracks in the darkened tunnels. The theater was rarely more than half full.

The films were quiet, subtle and often opaque. It was sometimes hard to tell which commandment was being addressed. The characters never spoke about the commandments directly. They were too busy, as we all are, coping with the duress of life. The stories presented the lives of ordinary people confronted by extraordinary events. All lived in a Warsaw housing complex, many of them neighbors, reinforcing the notion of our being on a common voyage, yet also out of touch with the pain and dislocation of those around us. The commandments, Kieslowski understood, were not dusty relics of another age, but spoke in important ways to the human predicament.

He dealt with the core violations raised by the commandments. He freed the commandments from the clutter of piety. The promiscuous woman portrayed in the film about adultery was not married. She had a series of carnal relationships. Adultery, for the director, was at its deepest level sex without love. The father in the film about honoring our parents was not the biological father. Yet the biological mother was absent in the daughter's life. Parenting, Kieslowski understood, is not defined by blood or birth or gender. It is defined by commitment, fidelity and love.

I knew the commandments. I had learned them at Sunday

school, listened to sermons based on the commandments from my father's pulpit and studied them as a seminarian. But watching Kieslowski turn them into living, breathing entities gave them a new resonance.

"For 6,000 years these rules have been unquestionably right," Kieslowski said of the commandments. "And yet we break them every day. We know what we should do, and yet we fail to live as we should. People feel that something is wrong in life. There is some kind of atmosphere that makes people turn now to other values. They want to contemplate the basic questions of life, and that is probably the real reason for wanting to tell these stories."[1]

In eight of the films there was a brief appearance by a young man, solemn and silent. Kieslowski said he did not know who he was. Perhaps he was an angel or Christ. Perhaps he represented the divine presence who observed with profound sadness the tragedy and folly we humans commit against others and ourselves.

"He's not very pleased with us," the director said.[2]

When our lives are shattered by tragedy, suffering and pain, or when we express or feel the ethereal and overwhelming power of love, we confront the mystery of good and evil. Voices across time and cultures have struggled to transmit and pay homage to this mystery, what it means for our lives and our place in the cosmos. No human being, no nation, no religion, has been chosen by God to be the sole interpreter of mystery. All cultures struggle to give words to the experience of the transcendent. This is the most powerful testament to the reality of God. It is a reminder that all of us find God not in what we know, but in what we cannot comprehend and cannot see.

These voices, whether in the teachings of the Buddha, the writings of Latin poets or the pages of the Koran, are part of our common struggle as human beings to acknowledge the eternal and the sacred. Nearly every religion has set down an ethical and moral code that is strikingly similar to the 10 Commandments.

The Eightfold Path, known within Buddhism as the Wheel of Law, forbids murder, unchastity, theft, falsehood and, especially, covetous desire. The sacred syllable "Om" for Hindus, said or sung before and after prayers, ends with a fourth sound beyond the range of human hearing. This sound is called the "sound of silence." It is also called "the sound of the universe." It is in the repetition of the Sacred Syllable that Hindus try to go beyond thought, to reach the stillness and silence that constitutes God. These are all constructs that the biblical writers would have recognized.

The more we listen to the voices of others, voices unlike our own, the more we remain open to the transcendent forces that save us from idolatry. The more we listen to ourselves, the more we create God in our own image until God becomes a tawdry idol that looks and speaks like us. The power of the commandments is found not in the writings of theologians, although I read and admire some, but in the pathos of human life, including lives that are very unlike our own. All states and nations work to pervert religions into civic religions, ones where the goals of the state become the goals of the divine. This is increasingly true in the United States. But once we believe we understand the will of God and can act as agents of God we become dangerous, a menace to others and a menace to ourselves. We forget that we do not understand. We forget to listen.

In 1983, I was in a United Nations camp for Guatemalan refugees in Honduras. Those in the camp had fled fighting. Most had seen family members killed. The refugees, when I arrived on a dreary January afternoon, were decorating the tents and wooden warehouses with colored paper. They told me they would celebrate the flight of Mary, Joseph and the infant Jesus to Egypt to escape the slaughter ordered by Herod of the children.

Why, I asked one of the peasants, was this an important day?

"It was on this day that Christ became a refugee," he answered.

I knew this Bible passage by heart. I had heard my father read it every year. But until that moment, standing in a muddy refugee camp with a man who may not have been able to read, I did not understand it. This passage meant one thing to me and another to parents who had swept children into their arms and fled to escape death. The commandments can only be understood in moments when they are no longer abstractions. Scholarship, especially biblical scholarship, divorced from experience is narrow, self-absorbed and frequently irrelevant. I learned more about this passage from a Salvadoran farmer than I ever could have from a theologian.

This book is about the lives of people, including myself, who have struggled on a deep and visceral level with one of the commandments. It came out of a series I wrote for *The New York Times*. Some of the stories in the series made it into the book, some did not. Those I write about, from Bishop George Packard, the former platoon leader in Vietnam, to R. Foster Winans, who went to prison for insider trading, cope with lives that have been turned upside down by an intense and overpowering experience with one of the commandments. There is nothing abstract about the commandments to those who know the sting of their violation or have neglected their call. It is this power I want to impart.

The commandments guide us toward relationships built on trust rather than fear. Only through trust can there be love. Those who ignore the commandments diminish the possibility of love, the single force that keeps us connected, whole and saved from physical and psychological torment. A life where the commandments are routinely dishonored becomes a life of solitude, guilt, anger and remorse. The wars I covered from Central America to Yugoslavia were places where the sanctity and respect for human life, that which the commandments protect, were ignored. Bosnia, with its rape camps, genocide, looting, razing of villages, its heady intoxication with violence, power and death, illustrated, like all wars, what happens when societies thrust the commandments aside.

The commandments do not protect us from evil. They protect us from committing evil. The commandments are designed to check our darker impulses, warning us that pandering to impulses can have terrible consequences. "If you would enter life," the Gospel of Matthew reads, "keep the commandments" (Matthew 19:17). The commandments hold community together. It is community that gives our lives, even in pain and grief, a healing solidarity. It is fealty to community that frees us from the dictates of our idols, idols that promise us fulfillment through the destructive impulses of constant self-gratification. The commandments call us to reject and defy powerful forces that can rule our lives and to live instead for others, even if this costs us status and prestige and wealth. The commandments show us how to avoid being enslaved, how to save us from ourselves. They lead us to love, the essence of life.

The German philosopher Ludwig Wittgenstein said, "Tell me 'how' you seek and I will tell you 'what' you are seeking."[3] We are all seekers, even if we do not always know what we are looking to find. We are all seekers, even if we do not always know how to frame the questions. This is what the commandments do for us. In those questions, even more than the answers, we find hope in the strange and contradictory fragments of our lives.

Chris Hedges
Princeton, New Jersey

MYSTERY

—◆—

You shall have no other gods before me.

I stand across from the Mission Main and Mission Extension Housing Project in Roxbury on a muggy July night. Scattered streetlights cast out dim yellow arcs on Parker Street. The remaining slate-gray metal poles, with their lamps shattered by rocks, leave the strip of asphalt gap-toothed, with lonely outposts of pale spotlights and long stretches of darkness. The unlit stretches are uncharted oceans of fear. They are filled with dangers imagined and real. At night, in the ghetto, I cling to light.

Parker Street is rutted and potholed. It rises and falls with the scars of old frost heaves. Newspapers, broken beer bottles, pieces of cardboard and plastic bags line the gutters. The triple-decker houses, cut into overcrowded apartments, are inhabited mostly with families from the Dominican Republic. The noise of people crushed together in small spaces, the shouts, the crying of children, the smell of fried food spill out into the street. Music with a Caribbean beat plays through several of the open windows.

The pale specter of television sets, the great Leviathan of modernity, the tool that teaches us to speak and think and cuts us off from our neighbors, sends out flickering images that reflect in the window panes. At night, striding up Mission Hill, it is often all I see, window after window, as if we are infected with a plague.

This has been my world for over two years. It will be my world
no more. I am leaving, leaving not only Roxbury but seminary,
leaving the church. I am turning on all that has formed me. I have
buckled under its weight. No more will I preach the Sunday sermons, sitting up late Saturday night as I write my words on yellow legal sheets. No more will I help carry in the coffins of those
I buried, lifting the thin strip of paper from the faces of the dead
when I open the box for viewing. No more will I ride the subway
to Cambridge to sit through seminars on theology or the psalms
or the Bible. No more will I divide up passages in the Hebrew
Bible with colored flares into the various sources identified by
scholars, the academic evisceration of the word. All this is over.

I heave an empty bottle against the wooden doors of the
Gloucester Memorial Presbyterian Church in Roxbury. The bottle splinters. I have watched children break bottle after bottle
against walls and pavement. Destruction is the way these children
affirm themselves, fight back against the forces above them.
These are weak, symbolic protests born of rage and pain. They
destroy. I sweep up. This is the pattern.

The long slow drip of oppression and abuse, which strips
human beings of dignity, was unknown to me until I moved to
the ghetto. I sympathize on this night with the rock throwers. I
sympathize although I spend hours every week removing the
signs of their pathetic protests. I know most will lose. I know the
ghetto will win. I know most of those born poor stay poor. And I
know I will protect myself if they turn on me. I can easily cross
the barrier that hems them in like sheep. I can turn to the instru-
ments of control and oppression—the police, the courts, the probation officers—for protection when I am afraid. I am not one of
them. I will never be one of them. I am the enemy.

I look at the shards of broken glass. I look at the hulking,
dimly lit red brick church. I look at the desolate holes of darkness
in the street, which always fill me with dread. All my dreams of
being an inner-city minister, all my illusions about myself, the

one who comes to save and care for others, the one who will be blessed and loved and honored for goodness, lie in little pieces on the ground. I have seen, through their eyes, the image of myself. It is not an attractive sight. It is not who I thought I was. It is not who I want to be.

"Now," I say softly, "I am on your side."

It is an act of apostasy. It is meant to mark my switch from the side of those who attend my church to those whom my tiny, dysfunctional congregation, although mostly African-American, look at with open disdain, those whom they dismiss as "the animals." It is meant to mark my break from institutions that overtly or subtly mete out oppression, including the various religious institutions that formed me. The breaking of the bottle is meant to be an ending, a final conclusion to a life spent in the powerful and claustrophobic embrace of the church. It is meant to be a break from God. But you trade one god for another. This is how life works. We all have gods.

Life is not lineal. We circle back to our origin, if not to embrace it then to understand how it shaped us, to examine with less heat and anger our marks and scars. As we age we pick through the disjointed shards and fragments of our existence. We try to piece them together into a coherent whole, these fragments of memory and identity, of happiness, of pain, of grief, of careers, of plans, of goals, of meaning, of relationships and of disillusionment, all these strange bits of colored glass, that make a life. We have been many people. When we examine the pieces, our own pieces, they seem odd to us, foreign to us as we hold them up into the light and try to puzzle out who we are and what we have become. We struggle to give them a coherency they do not possess.

We are a candle on a piece of polished steel. The steel, with its minute scratches, throws out graceful concentric, purposeful circles in the flickering light. These circles are an illusion, for no

matter where we move the candle the patterns always spread outward from the point of light. We delude ourselves with these patterns, as if our little flame is the center of something large and
important, as if the universe circles back to us, as if we are not
small and lost and confused.

These circles let us dream that we are especially blessed and
loved, that we deserve more than others and should cater to our
desires. We begin to give significance to things and experiences
that are no more significant than a countertop of random
scratches. But few of us want to shatter the illusion, to keep moving the candle until we see the artificial monuments we build to
ourselves. I feel small tonight on this street. I feel foolish for giving myself a purpose and place I had no right to envision. The
universe suddenly seems large and cavernous. I wonder if it
knows or cares I am here.

Insight in life comes through suffering, but suffering alone
does not bring insight. Many who suffer are trapped in the
venom of their own hate. They cannot forgive. They turn it back
on a world they despise. The hatred spawned by the abuser can
spread, without forgiveness, like a virus. It can leave the victims
imitating the brutality and intolerance. I see this in the ghetto.
Men, belittled and humiliated, return to the projects and mercilessly beat their wives and children. Domestic abuse is
widespread in my neighborhood. I have no romantic notions
about the poor. I have seen what abuse does to us. The belief that
because I have suffered I have a right to inflict suffering, is the
plague of the ghetto. There are few who rise above it, but those
who do have a nobility and dignity that sets them free. They do
not give in to the base impulses around them. They live by another code, a code that places compassion before revenge, a code
embodied in the commandments.

I arrived in Roxbury six days after graduating from Colgate
University. I had two heavy suitcases, packed with books, including a heavily underlined copy of Fyodor Dostoyevsky's *The Brothers*

Karamazov. The novel, dog-eared from rereading, helped send me into the ghetto. The talks and homilies of the Elder Zosima, as well as the discourse by the Grand Inquisitor, helped me ask the fundamental questions about the mystery of good and evil. The novel chronicles the spiritual death of those who dedicate their lives to the insatiable idols embodied in possessions and power, as well as intellectual and moral superiority.

> For the world says: "You have needs, therefore satisfy them, for you have the same rights as the noblest and richest men. Do not be afraid to satisfy them, but even increase them"—this is the current teaching of the world. And in this they see freedom. But what comes of this right to increase one's needs? For the rich, isolation and spiritual suicide; for the poor, envy and murder, for they have been given rights, but have not yet been shown any way of satisfying their needs. We are assured that the world is becoming more and more united, is being formed into brotherly communion, by the shortening of distances, by the transmitting of thoughts through the air. Alas, do not believe in such a union of people. Taking freedom to mean the increase and prompt satisfaction of needs, they distort their own nature, for they generate many meaningless and foolish desires, habits, and the most absurd fancies in themselves. They live only for mutual envy, for pleasure-seeking and self-display. To have dinners, horses, carriages, rank, and slaves to serve them is now considered such a necessity that for the sake of it, to satisfy it, they will sacrifice life, honor, the love of mankind, and will even kill themselves if they are unable to satisfy it. We see the same thing in those who are not rich, while the poor, so far, simply drown their unsatisfied needs and envy in drink. But soon they will get drunk on blood instead of wine, they are being led to that. I ask you: is such a man free? [1]

I lugged my suitcases down the steps to the subway station after getting off the bus, the moist heat dampening my white, pressed shirt. The sights and noises of the city were unfamiliar and disorienting. I boarded the Green Line and sat with the suitcases between my legs. I clutched a paper with the directions to the church.

"Why do you want to get off here?" the subway driver asked as I descended the steps onto Parker Street. He glanced warily toward the flat-roofed housing projects.

I did not have an answer. I muttered something vague about a job. I dragged the suitcases up Parker Street, which sliced through the center of the projects. I could have gotten off at the next stop, on Tremont, and avoided the sprawling projects, but did not know the landscape. Half moons of sweat formed under my armpits. The plastic handles of the suitcases bit into my fingers. I had to stop, leaving the suitcases flanking me, and then pick them up to move slowly forward. Men sat on the stoops and watched passively. The thin smoke from their cigarettes, held in their dark, nicotine-stained fingers, curled upward. Heat rose up from the concrete.

How curious it looked. A young man in a white button-down shirt, weighted down by two impossibly heavy suitcases, fighting his way up the middle of projects most white people did not enter. The eyes of the men followed me, silent, weary.

I found the manse behind the church. It lay between Parker and Gore Street. Gore Street was lined with vacant brick breweries, body shops, a wholesale Chinese fish warehouse and a few run-down houses. Gore Street was ill lit at night and largely deserted. It had the highest number of homicides in the city. Many buildings, blackened by fire, were boarded up, including the blue triple-decker building across the street. On one of the boarded-up windows were the words "fuck U" in spray paint.

The back windows in the manse were broken. The porch on the house, the roof covered with red asphalt shingles, looked as if it was about to collapse in the street, which it later did. The rosebushes had been dug up and stolen. Around the manse were small pits left by the thieves. The gates on the church playground, next to the house, had been removed. The basketball poles had been sawed down. Thieves had entered the church a few days earlier and stolen the cross, the baptismal font and the candle-sticks.

I went to the corner bodega and called one of the deacons. I read, sitting on the steps of the manse in the sun, until he arrived. He pulled up in an Impala about two hours later. I closed my book, got up, introduced myself and was given a key.

The manse was musty. It had been abandoned for six months. The mold in the refrigerator was overpowering. I held my breath to clean it. Shattered glass and a few rocks the size of baseballs lay on the floors in the empty rooms. Most of the windows had holes in them. The plaster was cracked and had gaping holes. The ceiling paint lay in large flakes on the floor. When I touched the woodwork it was black with dirt.

The first night I slept fitfully on a lumpy mattress in a second-floor room. The noises of the city, along with the groans of the barren eight-room house, kept me on edge. I got up at dawn, sun streaming in through the windows. I began to clean. I cleaned for four days. I had little money. I ate peanut butter on bread for breakfast, lunch and dinner. It was three weeks before I was paid.

I was hired by the church to work with inner-city youth. The program was funded by the regional offices of the Presbyterian Church. I was expected to preach most Sundays. I could not perform the sacraments of communion and marriage as a seminarian, but I could do most else, including funerals. I would bury seven people. But the congregation, which numbered no more than 15 or 20 people each Sunday, saw my chief role as protecting the property and warding off the neighborhood kids who had come close to stripping the buildings. The chairman of the trustee board—it seemed everyone in the congregation had a title and expected me to use it—arrived periodically to check my oversight. When the trash and broken windows outstripped my ability to clean and fix them he would tell me: "We let you live here for free. The least you could do is clean the place up."

Bricks were missing from the sidewalk in front of the church. Weeds pushed up through the cracks and rectangular spots of dirt. The sanctuary was in need of paint. Plaster had peeled off the wall and left huge, discolored patches. There were flakes of paint and plaster on the floor, as if the building was constantly shedding. There were holes in the stained glass windows where rocks had been thrown in from the street. A few of the windows, especially those along the street, had been covered with heavy plastic and plywood boards. Pigeons roosted on the high perches of the windows in the church. One of the deacons, to get rid of them, spent an afternoon playing his trumpet until the birds flew through the open windows to the street. The faded blue carpet was worn thin and had holes in the fabric. The pews were covered with dust.

The treasurer of the church was a portly woman in her midfifties. She ran the church like a fiefdom. She would bellow out to the congregation, moments after I had said the benediction, "No one leave your seats," and stride to the front of the church for "announcements." Her announcements could go on for half an hour, longer than my sermons.

I attended weekly church meetings that took up large chunks of my evenings in the hall next to the church. It was a low, two-story structure that had an open area with long tables, metal folding chairs and a large kitchen with a huge cast-iron black stove. The hall had been ransacked with repeated break-ins. Nearly everything, from Bibles to games to pots and pans, had been stolen.

Plans and programs were drawn up around a church that was, or would soon be, the focus of the community. Not long after I arrived it was decided that we would start a Sunday school. We had only one boy who attended church, and this on rare Sundays, with his grandmother. The lack of eligible children for a Sunday school, along with the fact that those who lived around us did not speak English, were Catholic or evangelicals, or more commonly had no interest in church at all, was not raised as an impediment.

We began a lengthy discussion about who would head the Sunday school, what books would be read, what time it would meet and whether the children would sit through part or all of the service.

"Should we look into bus service to pick the children up and then drop them off?" one of the deacons asked.

I looked at my watch. I had a mountain of work. If this did not finish soon I would be up past midnight. One of the deacons was told to draw up a cost estimate. I was told by the treasurer it was my job to find the kids and get them to come to church.

"We do a lot for these kids," the treasurer said. "The least they can do is come to the service. You work with them. Bring them to church."

I managed to get a few kids to come that Sunday. They sat bored and restless in the pew. They never came again. I could not blame them. There was nothing in the service that spoke to their reality or even acknowledged it.

On Christmas the treasurer brought a birthday cake to church. She paraded with the cake, topped with burning candles, down the aisle as those in the pews sang "Happy Birthday" to Jesus. She blew out the candles on Jesus' behalf. It was a ritual that caught me off guard the first year. I dreaded it the next. By the third year I was gone.

Hope and dignity, I soon saw, were stamped out by a complex web of city agencies and institutions that regarded the poor as vermin. I spent my first few weeks in despair. A boy about ten came to my door one morning and asked me to help his mother. We walked to her building, climbed the stairs that smelled of urine and pushed open the metal door of the apartment. The woman was lying on a couch. Her arm was raw with blood and her flesh torn from rat bites. She had fallen drunk on her floor and become a meal for rodents. The wounds were untended. She did not respond as I spoke to her. The child implored me to do

something. I found dish towels in the kitchen, which was filled
with dirty plates and filth, and wrapped them around the bites. I
lifted her onto the couch and left her, breathing heavily and
smelling of alcohol. I took her child to a neighbor.

A few weeks later, realizing how paltry my efforts would be, I
visited the Reverend Coleman Brown, the chaplain at Colgate. I
again sat in his corner office, the afternoon light slanting in
through the window, casting a golden hue over the cases of books,
books that had become familiar during my years as an undergrad-
uate. I asked Coleman, who had been a minister in East Harlem
and Chicago, if we were created to suffer.

"Is there any love that isn't?" he answered.

I remembered Dostoevsky asking "What is hell?" And his answering "The suffering of being no longer able to love."[2]

I grew up in a manse in Schoharie, a farm town in upstate New
York. It was a drafty white clapboard house built in 1801. It stood
on Main Street next to the red brick Presbyterian Church where
my father was the minister. I woke early on Sundays and traveled
with my father to churches in the outlying towns to hear him
preach. He would preach three times each Sunday to single or
consolidated congregations. We would discuss the sermon in the
car. The biblical stories shaped the way I saw the world. The poetry of the King James Bible gave me the cadences, rhythm and
images that fertilized my writing and my imagination. The Bible
with its stories of wickedness and magic, its great beasts, man-
swallowing whales, galloping horsemen, dead rising again to life,
is a work, to a boy, of startling surrealism.

The church was part of my daily rhythm. I look at the world
through the eyes it gave me. I spent evenings in church halls and
basements, eating potluck suppers prepared by elderly women
who flocked to the church and fussed over my father, my sister, my
brother and me. I folded bulletins on Saturday night and some-

times rapidly on Sunday morning. But I also knew the church's dark side, its self-righteous smugness, its crushing piety, the way it used religion to exalt itself and how it often masked human cruelty behind the quest for virtue and piety. Mark Twain said that an ethical man is a Christian holding four aces.[3] If you've got that you can afford to be ethical. Those I lived with in Roxbury had no aces.

I decided that July night in Roxbury not to be ordained. I decided I would have nothing to do with the church. I decided I would leave the United States for Latin America, where military regimes were suppressing popular dissent and death squads were dumping corpses on the roadsides. I would write about the conflicts in Argentina and El Salvador. I would give a voice to those who battled for social and political justice. It was as close as my generation would come to fighting fascism.

I decided many things. But in my youth, inexperience and anger, I did not understand that life has a way of deciding things for us. The themes and conflicts that define our lives are often not of our own choosing. We cannot pick our demons nor our angels. The anger toward the church, anger over its hypocrisy, anger over the way it treated its ministers, especially my father, anger over the way it treated me, did not free me to think or speak in another language. The fundamental questions, those formed within me by the church, would never change. And the questions, in the end, are what define us.

The ghetto, I soon learned, was also not done with me. It had one more lesson to teach. I intended to leave on my schedule, my time, but intentions are worth little. If you want to make God laugh, tell God your plans. There were my plans, but others, more powerful than I, had plans as well.

There were two teenage boys, Tyrone who was black and Patrick who was white, in my neighborhood. They did not attend school, although they were listed as students. Boston public schools had pupils, like these, on the books that had never been through their doors. These ghost students increased the allocated funds. Patrick and Tyrone could not read or write or tell time. They spent their days stealing car batteries that they sold for $5.00 to the local auto body shops. Patrick once stole $20.00 out of his father's wallet when his father was drunk. I saw him the next morning with David, the garage mechanic who bought his stolen batteries. They were eating at the small diner on Tremont Street where you could get eggs, bacon, hash browns and coffee for $2.00. He had taken David out to breakfast. Tyrone and Patrick were abused, neglected and unloved. Their alienation was so profound it was impossible, despite my efforts, to reach them. They lived in Dostoyevsky's hell of being unable to love.

Behind the manse was a dilapidated garage, which lacked doors. I found a brown plastic barrel in the garage. I dragged it out, got a broom and began to sweep the sidewalk the day after I arrived. I used a shovel to scoop up old cardboard crates, broken glass and newspapers and dump the trash in the barrel. I did not notice a group of teenagers watching with amusement. As I knelt to scoop another pile of broken glass onto the shovel and dump it in the barrel I heard the splintering sound of a bottle. I looked up the street and saw a large white boy, he must have been 170 pounds, grinning over the bits of glass. It was Patrick.

"Come sweep this up," he said.

The boys began to laugh.

I had come hoping to reach out to these kids, to build a relationship of trust and companionship. I wanted to be a minister. I should turn the other cheek. I swept it up as they watched. Moments later there was another crash of a bottle on the sidewalk. I swept that up. And then another. I shoved my broom and shovel into the barrel and went into the house, fighting to control my rage. When I returned the barrel had been dumped upside down.

I did not want the relationship they were forcing upon me. Why couldn't they see my good intentions? I had other visions for how I would be received, visions that had more to do with my own exaltation as a good person. I did not see yet that I represented the ordered, oppressive world they detested. I did not see my own culpability in that oppression.

I walked that night alone and saddened through the streets. When I came back to the church I found a small shark with its head smashed on the bricks. A chunk of cement, coated with blood, had been dropped repeatedly on the fish's head. The fish lay like a primal offering in front of the church door. The thought of boys, dropping the cement over and over on the head of this fish, disturbed me. It was one thing to kill it, but they had methodically smashed the head into a bloody pulp.

Tyrone, who was light-skinned, wiry and with freckles, stopped me the following morning.

"Me and Patrick stole the shark from the fish market," he said.

I had carted the fish off to the side of the church. It was surrounded by swarms of flies. I got my shovel, put the remains in a plastic bag and deposited it in my barrel.

I was outside the church a few days later, cleaning up as usual, and the group of boys came back for amusement. I was no longer polite. Patrick smashed a bottle, a grin creeping across his face. But this time I did not clean it up. I walked over to him, inches from his face, and told him to "fuck off."

I gave up on the litter and glass and garbage and went into the house. It was a gray, depressing afternoon. It began to rain. I sat on the edge of the mattress, the drops pelting the window glass. I put on my running shoes and shorts and ran in the rain to the Greater Boston YMCA, a few blocks from the projects. I lifted weights in the basement weight room and ran home.

The gym became my sanctuary, the only place I felt safe. The star of the weight room was a professional wrestler. He worked out with a midget who was his sidekick on the wrestling circuit. They arrived for their training sessions in a Cadillac. The midget, one afternoon, came alone. He did not have a key, which all of us who used the weight room had been issued after paying an extra fee. There was a banging on the door. One of the lifters opened the door, looked down the hall, saw no one as he glanced over the head of the midget, and slammed it shut.

"Hey," the midget yelled banging again, "let me in."

There were no windows in the weight room. Olympic weight bars and benches, many with the plastic covers torn and ripped, lay scattered about the room. There were piles of 45- and 35-pound metal plates on the floor. It smelled of close bodies and stale air. I rarely saw a woman. I arrived one evening that first summer and found the men in a foul mood with many throwing the round metal plates on the rubber mats.

I asked what was wrong.

"The price of blow jobs went up in the Combat Zone," a lifter told me.

"Damn whores," another said.

"Bitches," another added.

The boxers trained in the room next door. I watched them pound on the heavy bags, snorting out bursts of air through their nostrils, counting out their combinations in cadences. The rhythmic noises, the thuds of fists into the bags, provided a comforting drumbeat. The coach had been a ranked welterweight before being partially blinded when his cornea was scratched by old regulation gloves that had detached thumbs. He moved about the room in a windbreaker, exhorting his fighters, pushing them to fury. Thumbs, not long after his partial blinding, had been attached to gloves. But it came too late for him.

One evening he pulled white cotton wraps from the pocket on his blue windbreaker and wound the long strip of cloth around my wrists and hands. He helped me tie on a pair of red leather 16-ounce gloves.

"The first thing you have to learn is how to be hit and keep your eyes open," he said.

For the next two years, as my grades hovered one or two points above the line which would see me lose my scholarship at Harvard Divinity School, I found my community through him and his small group of fighters. We worked on the bags in the basement and sparred upstairs on the basketball court, slipping in our plastic mouthpieces and donning padded headgear. We had about a half dozen welterweight fighters who fought at 147 pounds. Quick and agile fighters frustrated me. They bobbed and wove beyond my touch. I was saved by my ability to absorb punches and by my strength. I enjoyed the punishment I inflicted when my blows connected with an opposing fighter and he began to reel, especially after I had been battered and outmaneuvered. This enjoyment, however, did not extend to hurting a dazed opponent.

One fighter, Jimmy, who had grown up in foster homes and was the only other white fighter, had large, thick hands. He was my size, with the exception of his wrists and fingers. His punches felt like cement. His blows sent shock waves through my body. My bones were not as large. I was conscious of this when I wound the cotton wraps around my palms. I suffered frequent sprains in my wrists. My hands always hurt. My girlfriend one night held my hand up in front of her and said: "Your wrists are thin." It was a moment when I felt that more than my bone structure had been exposed.

"My whole life is a lie," I answered.

The fighters clung to the sport. It was their last ticket out of a life of menial jobs in restaurants and on construction sites. Losses were not simply losses. They meant the end of the dream, the brutal realization that they would never escape from poverty and work they hated. The physical pain never matched the emotional collapse. Fighters, who rarely expressed emotion, buried their heads in their hands and wept, their shoulders shaking and their chests heaving, when they were crushed by an opponent. They disappeared soon afterward, often without saying good-bye. The pride, the cockiness, the arrogance, the hope, which could be insufferable, was suddenly swallowed up in despair. We greeted these defeats with silence. We offered weak words of encouragement. But we wanted them to go away. It was as if they had a disease we feared would infect us, a disease we knew to be mortal. It was defeat on this scale we feared most, more than the bruises, swollen ears and noses and blood that colored our urine.

We talked about champion fighters, how old they were when they got their break. We knew their fight styles and how these styles compared with our own. We modeled our boxing styles after those we emulated. Jimmy saw himself in Rocky Marciano, another young man, a cook, Sugar Ray Leonard. We came to believe we were these incarnations.

None of us talked about work. It was what you did to survive. Several of the fighters, including the coach, did construction. Some worked as cooks or in supermarkets. There was no glory or identity in profession. I did not have to explain that I was a divinity student. No one cared how I made a living. A few saw me cleaning up outside the church and assumed I was a janitor. I never corrected them.

When we finished sparring we ran five miles, sometimes along Parker Street. As we ran past groups of young men Jimmy would mutter, "I hope we get mugged."

The fights took place on Saturday night in Charlestown. We met at the gym and rode the subway with our gym bags on our laps. Prison buses, with wire mesh over the windows, delivered minimum security prisoners in handcuffs and leg shackles. They were brought as part of the prison's recreation program. Few of us stood a chance against the inmates. The inmates covered up long fight records to box as amateurs. Some came from New York and Philadelphia, which for some reason made them appear more intimidating. They worked out hours every day. They rarely had mercy when their opponents, stunned from a combination, stumbled backward. The local fighters from Charlestown, all white, were much less menacing. The crowds came to life when there was blood and dazed fighters. They shouted for the inmates to knock us down. "Hit him! Hit him!" the crowd would bellow. I swiftly realized this was a good way to get hurt and decided early in my career to spend my time during the Saturday bouts working the corner.

The arena was dimly lit. It had a boxing ring surrounded on all four sides by metal folding chairs. We were paid $25.00 a fight whether we won or lost. Those who came to watch were older men, who smoked and drank beer. Charlestown was an ugly place. The crowd shouted out racial slurs. The white sections of Boston, such as Charlestown, were far more dangerous for a black man than Roxbury was for a white. There may have been more violent crime where we lived, but there was much more hate in the white enclaves in the city. Most in my neighborhood would not drive a car through South Boston. Walking down a street in a place like Charlestown, even during the day, was out of the question.

The crowd had sympathy only for winners. I watched the crowd boo and jeer a fighter one night who was overweight, ridiculing him mercilessly with insults as he warmed up in the corner. The bell rang and he began to fight with tenacity and speed. He overwhelmed his opponent. The crowd began to cheer and whistle. They shouted encouragement and applauded his victory. It was always like this. You swung between hatred and glory, often within seconds of each other. It was a world without compassion.

Once a fighter was dazed, especially one of our own, we implored the referee to stop the fight. Boxing as a sport was fine, beating up a dazed kid who was having his body and his dream pummeled into the ground was not. We hated boxing then, hated the crowd, the anger, the intensity, everything about it. But it was the blood and the destruction of young men, maybe even the destruction of their dreams, that the crowd paid money to see. The fight went on until the victim tumbled onto the canvas.

I had the wind knocked out of me in one bout. I struggled to draw gulps of air, high-pitched gasps coming out of my lips. My opponent, startled by the sound, backed away.

"Hit him," the referee said. "The fight's not over."

"Yes it is," I choked out, holding up my hands and walking to the corner.

"You don't have enough hate in your heart to be a boxer," the coach told me afterward.

I began to sour on the sport. I clung to the camaraderie, a camaraderie that I did not want to give up for the loneliness and fear in the projects. But I went home after fights or practices with my head swimming. I felt seasick. I lay on my bed, ice wrapped in a cloth on my forehead. I lay as still as possible trying to focus when I opened my eyes, the ceiling spinning above me. I hated this more than the pain and bruises and bloody urine. It could be hours before my vision returned.

One night we were in the gym sparring. A group of college women were having an exercise class on the basketball court. They were probably from Northeastern University. To the other boxers they were beyond reach, these girls with lithe bodies and high school diplomas and fine manners. I peered back at my world.

"Come on," Jimmy said as we got ready to spar, "I'll make you look good."

I began to skip workouts after two years. My heart was not in it. I put on the heavy gloves, always slightly moist inside, during one of my last workouts. We began to spar. Jimmy did not hit me in the head. He glowered at me during the break. We began again. Again, he did not hit me in the head.

I took out my mouthpiece.

"Why don't you hit me in the head?" I asked.

Jimmy and a couple other fighters crowded in on me.

"You're studying to be a pastor," he said. "We will never hit you in the head again. We are dumb fucks. You need your mind for the Lord."

I had packed away my button-down shirts. I had grown my hair and tied it in a ponytail. I wore an old leather jacket. I had seen enough of the ghetto to fear that there would come a day when I would have to fight, to play by the code of the street. Boxing for me was also about survival. I tried to build relationships with Patrick and Tyrone, inviting them to the house for dinner, but it was doomed. I could not reach them. Tyrone lived with his mother, a drug addict. He often came home and was locked out of the apartment. He would pound on the door and she, passed out, would not answer. He spent nights sleeping outside the door, curled up like a dog. He did not know his father. Patrick's father was brutal, a well-built man who worked on the maintenance crew at Harvard. He had little use for his sons.

I was walking across Harvard Yard one morning on the way to a class after Dartmouth students had poured a bucket of green paint over the statue of John Harvard, seated imperiously in his chair. Patrick's father was one of the maintenance men in green uniforms cleaning the paint. I turned swiftly to walk the other way, my back to him, deeply embarrassed, not wanting him to see me.

I connected with Tyrone only once, when I gave him a picture I had taken of him. He had never seen a picture of himself. He looked at me for the first and only time without hatred.

"I will put it up over my bed," he told me.

It made no difference. It did not halt the slide to our inevitable confrontation. As I moved ploddingly around the ring, stepping forward to try and hit Jimmy, his face encased in headgear, I knew I was practicing for more than a $25.00 fight in Charlestown. There would soon come a time when, playing by new rules, I would use all I had learned in the gym.

On a dismal rainy afternoon, running to the gym, I was at the end of Alfonso Street. I heard a banging on a window above me. It was Edgar. He was waving. He spent his afternoons with some other kids, playing board games like Chutes and Ladders in my house. It was one of those moments where the sun burst through, where it seemed to be all worth it. There were not many. I waved back.

The administration at Harvard Divinity School took a dim view of my decision to live and work in Roxbury. They had given me a full scholarship, but not, in the words of a dean, "to be a social worker." I was told I had to maintain a B average or I would lose my scholarship. Most semesters I barely made it. I devoted my time to the ghetto. I missed my classes Friday to go with kids from the neighborhood to juvenile court. I preached on Sundays. I let the kids have the run of my house. There was the sweeping and cleaning around the church. At night, after practice, I sat drinking coffee in the gloomy manse, trying to concentrate on the writings of early church fathers or dense books of theology.

My relationship with Tyrone and Patrick deteriorated. They taunted me openly in the street. An encounter was looming, an encounter the neighborhood waited for with interest.

Patrick and Tyrone came and asked me for some matches one afternoon. They said they wanted to get high. I gave them matches. A few minutes later they were back at my door.

"Hey, man," Patrick said, "you missing some keys on a red key chain, 'cause I know who took them."

I put my hand on my pocket. I had left them in the door.

"Yeah," I said. "I guess I am."

"These kids from the projects have them," Tyrone said.

"You give us a reward if we bring um back?" Patrick asked.

"How much you want?" I said.

"A buck apiece," Patrick said.

"All right," I said.

They left on their bikes. In a few minutes they brought the keys back, minus the key chain and one key, the key to the church.

I could not start my car a few days later. My gas line had been cut. My motor mount had been sawed off. As I was looking under the car Patrick and Tyrone appeared on their bikes and smirked at my distress.

"What's wrong with your car?'" Patrick said.

"Get the hell out of here," I said.

I got up and pushed Patrick backward. He fell on the road. I picked him up and threw him against the fence. He was shaken. It was the first time I had been violent. I turned my back to them, went into the house. There was gasoline on my shoes and engine grease on my hands.

"Bastards," I said, and put my fist through the plaster wall in the hallway.

A police car stopped outside. The cops looked at the puddle of gas and asked if they could help. I knew most of them.

"Listen," one said gently, "you are not going to get anywhere by being nice. When you are nice it is weakness."

We had a guest preacher that Sunday. All I had to do was read the scripture. His sermon was terrible, one of those messages of love and reconciliation that have no relation to the world a few feet away. He did not live here. I listened to him with annoyance. I told him what happened to my car and how I reacted after the service.

He looked at me and said:

"When your enemies destroy your goods, rejoice."

I said nothing. I wanted to suggest he park his family car in the projects for a night. His response symbolized for me how out of touch liberal theology is with the world, blunted by too many years catering to the comfortable in affluent suburban churches, rendered hollow by platitudes and the naiveté of the pampered and protected.

"Many wealthy or suburban Christians would be appalled," I wrote that night in my journal. "From the comfort of a spacious living room they would talk of nonviolence and Christian love. I am afraid they are the only group that can keep such absurdities alive. A practicing Christian in Roxbury knows that one can no longer practice their faith if they are broken, and the only way not to be broken is to set boundaries. Martin Luther King walked from Montgomery to Memphis because a detachment of National Guardsmen walked with him. Society is not based on love but coercion."

The encounter with Patrick disturbed me.

"All night I hated myself," I wrote, "for pushing a fifteen-year-old punk who gets beaten up by his parents. What future do Patrick and Tyrone have? None I guess, a future of hate until we snuff them out. They mirror the destruction we have done to them. When we see Frankenstein rear his head we flee until we are forced to kill our creation."

A few days later the phone lines were cut. It was late October. I would soon begin to hear from the deacons complaints about my heating bill. The house, poorly insulated and large, leaked heat like a sieve. I knew who cut the lines, but I was not upset. I hated the telephone. It gave me a few days of peace.

While I could not reach Patrick and Tyrone, I could reach others. There was one boy, Stanley, nicknamed Junior, who had the best chance of making it out of the projects. Junior, who was 16, was huge. He weighed over 200 pounds, and constantly perspired. I nagged him to shower and bought him deodorant. He had a thick, heavy Afro and open smile. His mother, who worked two jobs, kept their small apartment clean and neat.

Stanley carried a knife with a six-inch blade. It was the biggest in the neighborhood. His bulk, along with his knife, meant people left him alone. It was Stanley who warned me about Patrick and Tyrone. Patrick had offered to trade his bike for Stanley's knife.

"I asked him why he wanted my knife," Stanley said, "and he told me he was going to kill someone. He was going to kill a white person. I didn't trade it for his bike. I was afraid he would stab you."

We were moving toward a clash. I could have obtained a knife, but did not, hoping that two years of boxing had left me agile and strong. I knew my fate would be determined in the first few seconds when they reached for their knives.

On hot nights I lugged a mattress down the stairs to the dining room. It was the only room in the house that had an air conditioner. The heavy old machine rattled and shook, emitting a thin stream of tepid air.

I lay on the floor one night, a thin sheet covering me, and heard a girl shouting in the alley between the manse and the church. She screamed. I leapt up, hastily pulled on my jeans and sneakers, and ran outside. Patrick and Tyrone were ripping the clothes from a 12-year-old girl. I seized Patrick from behind and threw him on the cement. I did the same with Tyrone. I moved quickly to keep them from pulling their knives from their pockets.

I did not hit them. I lifted them up and threw them on the cement until, bruised and asking me to stop, they promised to leave.

"You are not allowed on my street," I shouted as I picked the girl up off the ground. "Don't ever try and walk on my street again." I walked her home and handed her over to her brother, who was not much older. Her mother, a prostitute, was at work.

I knew Patrick and Tyrone would be back. I knew there would be no reconciliation. I knew they could not afford to lose face. And I knew I was an easy target. It did not take long for them to challenge me. It came the next day. They stood with their bikes on the far end of the street.

"Hey," Patrick said. "We are on your street."

He turned the word "your" into a sneering taunt.

I did not want to confront them, but I had no choice. Several other kids watched us passively. I walked toward the two boys. They turned, laughing, and rode away. A few days later I passed them sitting on the steps with about a half dozen other kids. Tyrone flipped me the finger. I wanted to pretend that I did not see him, but I stopped the car and waded through the other kids until I was close to his face.

"You got some business with me?" I asked.

"No," he said.

I could confront Tyrone because I was from the neighborhood. The confrontation was personal. If an outsider had done the same thing, especially a white man, he would have had to take on the group. But this was a private battle. Revenge became paramount. They boasted in the street that they would kill me.

I came home one afternoon to find the lock of my door smashed. I walked into the hall, nervous about finding someone inside. My small stereo was gone, along with my bike and my alarm clock. The stack of board games I had bought for the kids had been taken. The pile of old black choir robes, which the kids used to put on to be Japanese warriors, lay in a heap on the floor. I knew who had broken inside. I tracked down the neighborhood children. I threatened to leave, to move that night if they did not tell me who entered the house. Several started to cry. I gathered enough witnesses to call the police and take Patrick and Tyrone to court.

It was Officer Joe who arrived to investigate. He was a white police officer who lived in the neighborhood. He was married to a black woman. He wore his sadness and compassion on his face. He took notes for the report, speaking to those who had seen the break-in.

"I used to do what you're doing with these kids," he said. "I don't do it anymore. I can't. I don't know, I don't know . . ."

His voice trailed off to a whisper.

There was a can of turpentine on the stairs. Patrick, I was told by another boy, planned to burn down the house but was talked out of it. The lives of the two teenagers had become desperate. They sold blow jobs to get money for heroin. They stole cars, driving the vehicles recklessly through the streets. Late one night they plowed an Oldsmobile into a porch. The crash woke the neighborhood. I saw them climb out of the car and run. Tyrone was limping and yelling "Oh, shit! Oh, shit! Oh, shit!" They rarely went home and lived together in an empty house. It had no running water. They passed threats along through the kids on the street.

"We are going to jump Chris from behind with baseball bats."

"We are going to knock out the windows on his car."

"We are going to burn his house down with him in it."

I was angry now, determined to destroy them with the levers of the system that had deformed them. It was my system. It protected me. I knocked down the padlocked door of their room in the abandoned house. I found an old space heater, some plastic milk cartons for stools and a cot. I took the fuses out of their fuse box. I called the police to evict them. I bought plywood and boarded up the windows of their sanctuary. I called their mothers. I filed complaints with their probation officers. I had court orders that demanded they pay restitution for the property they stole. I told them if they ever touched me, or any of the kids who had testified against them, I would beat them into a pulp. I went home after these brief confrontations and paced the house, shaking, nervous, afraid.

"They watch me," I wrote of Patrick and Tyrone, "as I come back from school with piles of books and half-read newspapers under my arm. They see something they despise. It is the advantage of wealth, education and race. It is the advantage of money enough to be honest, to be decent."

I went to court with my brood of witnesses. I wore a suit with a white shirt and tie in court. I crossed deftly into the world of college-educated men and women. I spoke like the lawyers, the same grammatically correct English. Patrick and Tyrone glared at me, angry, sullen. I looked at them and wondered about the notion, so common in seminary, that we are all made in the image of God. They responded, as far as I could tell, to only one emotion—fear. Their souls had been twisted into an unfathomable maze of anger, resentment and self-destruction.

We do not choose the forces that create us, the forces at home, at school, in our community. These forces mold or condemn us. They tie us to a class or cast us out as human refuse. These boys had never known love. They had been beaten, abused and neglected. I represented what they had been denied. There was no justice. The world around them conspired to destroy them. The noise, the overcrowding, the poverty, the abuse, the indifference of the courts and the schools and the overburdened probation officers doomed them. But the most destructive force was living without love.

I stood on an October afternoon in Patrick and Tyrone's abandoned house with a police officer. The boards had again been removed from the windows. The wind whipped across the vacant lot. We stomped our feet on the rotting wood. I wanted to have them arrested.

"Looks like they're not here," the cop said.

He wore a heavy gun belt and a black leather jacket. He had a narrow black tie that was clipped onto his blue collar. He was staring out the window. It was a while before he spoke.

"You know it's not these kids' fault," he said. "They never get a chance."

The leather in his belt creaked slightly. We walked down the stairs, the steps groaning under our feet, of the old house, built a century ago by the German immigrants who came to work in the breweries. I pictured the nights they had sat in the kitchen, their burdens and dreams, the children who had been tucked into beds, the fragility of their lives and hope for the future now long forgotten.

"It's all bluff," he said when we got outside. "Any seventeen-year-old on this block could lay me flat. I came here to help these people. Now I do it to put bread on the table."

The radio crackled from inside his patrol car. He got in and drove away. I walked back to the church.

I sat with Patrick and Tyrone on the steps of an abandoned house a few days before they tried to kill me. They were high on heroin, their eyes glassy, their gaze distant, far away. They spoke slowly, heavily, the words rolling out of their mouths with difficulty. I could leave and find a place in the world. They could not.

The white powder in a plastic baggie was their only escape, the only way to dull the pain, despair and fear for a couple of hours. It was a god, their god. We think these gods will serve us, but they turn out to enslave and destroy us.

I was not sure they knew I was present. I stayed for a while, silent, sad. I knew what would happen. I knew where the three of us were headed. This would be our last communion. My only hope came now in departing the ghetto before they had time to act.

Patrick and Tyrone were using a lot of heroin. They would shoot up in alleys or the abandoned house. They sat motionless, often for hours, on the steps of the building across the street. Their thefts and robberies were brazen. They stole cars, sometimes resisting the urge to sell them to set them ablaze in dramatic nighttime displays of rage. Great bursts of flame shot up on deserted streets, sending startled sleepers to windows and fire trucks to hose down the flames.

I was ready to leave. I was tired of the work, sick of the ghetto, disenchanted with the church and seminary. I had attacked my idol on the steps of the church. My mind was elsewhere, in South America where I was going to study Spanish at the language school run by Maryknoll, the Catholic missionary society. I planned my departure.

I came home one afternoon at dusk and parked my Volkswagen in front of the house. I gathered up my piles of books from the passenger seat and climbed the steps to the front door. I heard movement behind the door and opened it cautiously. It was Stanley. He was seated on the stairs, his open knife next to him. He was crying.

"You better get out of here," he said. "I found Patrick and Tyrone with pipes. They were waiting to kill you."

Stanley took me to the kitchen. The back window was smashed, glass shards lay on the cracked linoleum floor. Tyrone and Patrick had climbed in through the kitchen. They were waiting in the hall when Stanley came up behind the house. Stanley had hoisted himself inside and confronted them.

I sat down on the steps next to Stanley. This was the end. I would never sleep here again. We packed up a few of my things. I began to call friends, searching for a couch or space on a floor. I would live like this for weeks, lying awake at night in Cambridge or Brighton or Allston in strange apartments, counting down the days until I departed.

I was finished with the ghetto. I was finished with the church. I went through the motions at Harvard. I returned after a year in South America to finish my degree, but lived close to Cambridge. I went to class, studied and went home again. I did not get ordained. The degree was completed because it had been begun. I left for El Salvador when I graduated as a freelance reporter to cover the war.

All this was a long time ago. It was a time I dreamed of being good. But this was the idolatry of self, the worship not of God but of my virtue. I had to learn my own complicity in oppression, my own sinfulness, how evil lurked within me, how when I was afraid I could turn on the weak and powerless.

Where are they now, these pot washers and construction workers who thought for a brief moment they were Sugar Ray Leonard? Where are these boys on Parker Street who destroyed everything around them as they were destroyed? Where are the theology professors, wrapped in the narcissism of their own scholarship, who spoke of liberation and empowerment for the poor, but who never went to the ghetto?

The darkness I discovered in Roxbury was my darkness, our darkness. It is what I carried out of the ghetto, onto the platform at Harvard when I received my diploma, into the thin ribboned stretch of Central America, the refugee camps in Gaza, the UN feeding stations in the southern Sudan and the cold, murderous streets of Sarajevo. It is knowledge of this darkness that alone makes faith possible. The church was my last refuge from God. In the shattering of that moral certitude I looked for forgiveness. Idols promise us power. God does not. Before God we all are powerless. We are all afraid. It is in this fear, this darkness, that I found God, even as I thought I was fleeing God. I abandoned the institutions that claimed God's authority. I walked down Parker Street the night I smashed that bottle on the church doors, leaving the light, and entering "the thick darkness where God was."

IDOLS

You shall not make for yourself a graven image, or any likeness of anything that is in heaven above, or that is in the earth beneath, or that is in the water under the earth; you shall not bow down to them, or serve them.

At one point, all that mattered in Beth Senturia's life was the band. She lived like a nomad, hitching rides from one Phish concert to the next, living off what she could sell in the parking lot before a concert and taping performances to capture the events for rock-and-roll posterity.

"I am a taper," she said when I met her one rainy winter's night in New York. "I am Moses bringing the music down from the mountain."

She dropped out of Barnard College, never to go back. She could not hold down a job, quitting each time the band went on tour. She became a "tour head." She spent weeks on the road and saw, by the time she was done, 207 shows. She fell into drugs, the vagabond lifestyle, casual relationships and then crashed.

"There are parts of their music that can be a spiritual experience," she said, "but at the same time it can be very easy to make that experience idolatrous. It can remove you from the real world. It can become a cult."

Phish, a Vermont jam rock band that had a following similar to the Grateful Dead, exuded a powerful pull on her and thousands of others. "Phish heads" constructed a subculture, a way of life, where the music and the concerts shut out the rest of the world. "Trey is God" read a bumper sticker sold at concerts before the group disbanded, a message not completely in jest. Trey Anastasio was the band's lead guitarist.

"I have to be careful that I do not drop everything and go out on the road again," said Senturia, now in her thirties and working for a financial services firm. "I do not need to run from my life anymore."

The concert experience resembled worship, a spiritual encounter. It thrust her into the present and at its most exalted moments was rapturous. It removed her from ordinary life. It left her with feelings of transcendence. She found in the concerts something she was unable to find anywhere else. All of life, work, school, relationships were sacrificed to follow the band. She found an identity in the band. She locked out everything that intruded on the experience.

The danger of idolatry runs through every commandment. But warding off the allure of idols is difficult. The God of the Bible is ineffable, unknowable, hidden. The mystery frustrates and defies us. To worship God, it seems, is to worship nothing. There is no security. Belief in a God we cannot know seems to leave us stranded on an island of insecurities. God is not like the tangible things we can have faith in, not like our idols. Idols comfort us, reassure us and empower us. They can be understood. Idols appear, when we worship them, to give us what we want. It is easier to have idols. It is harder to trust in the unknown, in the darkness, in the voice answering Moses' request for revelation with the words: "I AM WHO I AM."[1]

God cannot be summed up in a name. God cannot be described. Only idols provide this certitude. But watch, God seems to say, you will know me when you encounter me. You will see who I am in the profound flashes of self-knowledge that cut through darkness, in the hope that rises out of despair and suffering, in the loving touch of another, in a moral life where we resist the worship of ourselves so others can prosper. God, the experience of God, is real. Poets, painters, composers and writers have struggled for centuries to express this mystery. It is what prophets and religious thinkers, from Buddha to Moses to Mohammed, describe and revere. Those who sanctify their own power deny this mystery. They promise that God can not only be known but also manipulated. False prophets, who say they can harness the power of God for us, lead us away from the worship of God into the corrosive idolatry of self-worship. They seek to speak not only for God, but for the nation, fusing religion and nationalism into a dangerous brew that brings us to kneel before the idol of the state.

We are burdened by household gods, no longer made of clay, but all promising to fulfill us. Our computer, our television, our job, our wealth, our social status, along with the brands we wear and the cars we drive, promise us contentment and inform our identity. These household gods seem to offer well-being, health and success. But all these gods create cults. And all these cults circle back to us, to a dangerous self-worship fed by forces who seek to ensnare us in idolatry.

We can see the idols others worship. It is hard to see our own. We depend on our idols to give us order and meaning. We depend on our idols to define our place in the world. Idols give us a world that appears logical and coherent. Idols free us from moral choice. Idols determine right and wrong. Idols render judgment. We follow. We conform.

When we see the hollowness of our idols, how they have led us to waste time and energy, when we smash these false gods and peer at the uncertainty of life, those who continue to revere the idol turn against us. We are expelled from the cult, stripped of its identifying power and left alone. It is easier to remain silent, to pay homage to a false god even after this god is exposed as a fraud. Those who worship idols deal harshly with those who become apostates.

The idols of nation, race, religion, ethnicity, gender and class are idols that demand exclusive and false covenants. These covenants exalt ourselves, as long as we only define ourselves through these narrow definitions, and exclude others outside the circle. Idols are always about self-worship. The idols subvert the equality that protects us from tyranny and injustice, the respect that urges us to see the worth and dignity in all human life, even in those who oppose us. But the fear of exclusion, of incurring the wrath of those who worship the idol, sees us willing to justify the ostracism and even abuse of others.

We are joined together, Augustine wrote, as a community by our love of the same object. Human love, he wrote, is always directed either toward God or the self. There are no other choices. The other loves we have in life, the love of status, the love of possessions, the love of power, are always the love of self. We have, Augustine argued, two choices in life. We can embrace the City of God, where we struggle to love to the exclusion of the self, a love that forces us to negate ourselves and our security to conserve, preserve and protect others, or we can embrace the City of Man where unbridled self-interest makes us all enemies. In the City of God, where we make hard and sometimes painful sacrifices for others, we become part of a whole. In the City of Man, where we live only for advancement of the self, we become part of a mob. The commandments, when followed, keep us in the City of God. When violated they exile us to the City of Man.

Those who place their faith in idols seek to flee from the hard demands of the City of God. They seek a larger self, a way to rise above the ordinary, a way to defeat these uncertainties and insecurities. Idols create sacred space around them. They assume the mantle of the divine. They appear to be God. The follower of idols engages in worship that appears to be real and authentic.

"For us it is like going to synagogue or church," said Loren Bidner, 24, about Phish. "It is cathartic. We are in touch with ourselves, our thoughts and our experiences."

Anastasio, with his band softly playing in the background, frequently related mythological tales during the concerts from Gamehenge, a fantasy world he created. The stories were about the "Helping Friendly Book," which existed in Anastasio's imagination. The lessons from the book were intended to "help the people of Gamehenge live in peace." Anastasio, who mixed in songs with the story, could spend 90 minutes telling the audience his elaborate tales about the destruction of a peaceful culture by the evil tyrant Wilson and the revolution that eventually overthrew him. The last song at the end of the cycle saw the revolutionary leader begin to evolve into another tyrant.

The "Helping Friendly Book" was said to contain "the ancient secrets to eternal joy and everlasting splendor," or so goes a line from the song "Lizards," part of the cycle. The song continued, "The trick was to surrender to the flow."

The emotional pull of the band, with its own peculiar mythology, created a dependence Senturia and many others could not break. When the band took its first break from touring, before finally breaking up, bumper stickers appeared that read, "Trey is Wilson."

Yet within the music and the lyrics were wild contradictions. Songs about maiming, violence and death were sung to happy, up-tempo beats. The songs ridiculed the sanctity of life and the consequences of violence. Moral purpose became, in the hands of the band, a joke, absurd. The music and the message resembled the absurdity of Dadaism, the nihilistic protest movement that sprung up among artists after World War I. It too was a movement in rebellion against depersonalization and mechanization, especially mechanized mass killing. But like the culture of war it was reacting against, it made the fatal mistake of ridiculing all values. Dadaism, like the band, fused contradictions to brand all moral systems empty.

"The attraction to Gamehenge is similar to the attraction to *Star Trek,*" Senturia said. "It is a world where everyone can live in peace in the future if they get the book back from the evil King Wilson. Yet when you look at the message it calls for different reactions to life. One must go with the flow yet fight evil. It does not always make sense."

The lyrics provoked long debate among Phish followers. Many collected amateur tapes of concerts and the set lists of each concert. They tried to decipher the order of songs for hidden messages. They referred to fellow concertgoers as their "Phish family." They found meaning in the music, as well as in the fantasy stories. They learned to speak in Phish code, a language full of terms that allowed the initiated to communicate and locked out nonbelievers.

"If you look at what we might idolize it is not one of the guys in the band," Bidner said. "We are not going to see Trey or Mike. We are going for something that is much bigger than the four of them. It is much bigger than one instrument. It is a subculture. We become nomadic, traveling with packs of friends."

Physical and emotional distances vanished during the concerts. The crowd became a living, breathing organism as long as it was able to direct its energy and focus toward the communal, emotional highs and lows. This communal experience gave the illusion of equality, belonging and insight. They felt removed from the outside world, lifted above the common herd, initiated into another way of being.

The crowd is the tool all idols use to perpetuate themselves. Crowds are always dangerous, for they enforce conformity, impart a feeling of power and false equality, focus attention on an object or person, and do not tolerate dissent. Crowds seek out idols to venerate. Any attempt to defy the crowd, which takes on a life and identity, can be dangerous. Dissenters, rare and infrequent, are ruthlessly crushed. The crowd experience offers a transcendence that is powerful and attractive.

The experience of belonging to the crowd appeared to give to followers a new, vibrant community, even as it destroyed community. The self-absorption and moments of ecstasy turned those on the outside, those who did not worship the idol, into a hostile, even evil force. The private mythology and slang offered elaborate verbal mechanisms and private rituals to separate from the uninitiated. There were growing feelings of persecution. There was open contempt for those outside the "Phish family." Those in the crowd grew afraid, afraid of all forces which threatened the experience. They began to interpret all forces as bent on their destruction. They grew suspicious of each other.

The devotion to the band, the drugs, the concerts, the nomadic, restless existence, perpetuated not so much childhood, as some thought, but childishness. They subscribed to a naive and dangerous optimism, based not on responsibility and sacrifice, but on a simplistic belief that if they felt good everyone should feel good. The longer they fled, the more they folded into this world, the more self-righteous, intolerant and finally angry they became. They sought, over and over, what the band, what all idols cannot give: permanent rather than transitory meaning. A life dedicated to transitory happiness is poisonous and impossible to maintain.

Phish followers told me they did not take the long elaborate stories about Gamehenge seriously, but that was precisely the point. They confused cynicism with sophistication. The cynicism was an excuse for irresponsibility and self-centeredness. They took nothing, other than the transcendent experience, seriously. Life was reduced to a desperate effort to recreate fleeting moments of ecstasy. Life was lived in the pursuit of a momentary high; all else was rejected and ridiculed. They did not seem to be aware that they were replicating patterns within the larger soci-

ety, patterns they thought they were rejecting, patterns of longing, of a thirst for sensual gratification at the expense of others.
They ignored problems or injustices that did not touch them directly.

The childishness of the Phish followers reflected our own
childishness, our belief that if we are happy, if we are entertained
and feel good, then the rest of the world will take care of itself.
Others should find a way to feel good with us. We abandon our
mentally ill to sleep on city heating grates, leave children in urban
ghettos functionally illiterate, scuttle our public transportation
system, deny 45 million of our citizens health insurance and scrap
controls on coal-burning power plants that poison the air and
water supply. We fail to examine what is done in our name in
countries such as Iraq and Nigeria. We go along with the flow,
deadened to the pain of others, seeking our own emotional transcendence. The world will take care of itself.

Dietrich Bonhoeffer, who ran an underground theological
seminary during Nazi rule in Germany and was put to death after
being implicated in a plot to kill Adolf Hitler, particularly feared
the childish, the foolish. He saw in their folly a dangerous escapism. He argued that their indifference to moral choice left
them unable to discern between good and evil, unable to act, unable to care. It left them paralyzed. He feared the paralysis of the
foolish for it made evil possible. It is the foolish who allow evil to
triumph. Devoted to self-satisfaction, they do not react when
open societies are subverted. They retreat further, like the Phish
followers, into their escapism. They label all values as absurd;
they cannot see, until it is too late, that some values are worth
fighting to preserve, that losing these values makes even private
contentment impossible.

"Folly is a more dangerous enemy to the good than evil," wrote
Bonhoeffer. "One can protest against evil; it can be unmasked
and, if need be, prevented by force. Evil always carries the seeds
of its own destruction, as it makes people, at the least, uncom-

fortable. Against folly we have no defense. Neither protests nor
force can touch it; reasoning is no use; facts that contradict personal prejudices can simply be disbelieved—indeed, the fool can
counter by criticizing them, and if they are undeniable, they can
just be pushed aside as trivial exceptions. So the fool, as distinct
from the scoundrel, is completely self-satisfied; in fact, he can
easily become dangerous, as it does not take much to make him
aggressive."[2]

We are tempted and often encouraged to retreat, to hide in
the little sanctuaries we build around idols. We believe these idols
will protect us, never realizing that idols are always willing to sacrifice their own, to ensure their own preservation. As the world
around us becomes bleaker all acts of resistance seem futile. Cynics remind us of their insignificance. But acts of compassion affirm life in the face of death. These acts hold at bay the crippling
power of death and despair. They allow us to live, allow us to be
human, allow us to affirm others and ourselves. When we do not
accept pain as an inevitable part of life, when we are no longer
willing to sacrifice, we embrace death and reject life.

Resistance defeats nihilism. It is the only way to rescue and
maintain meaning. The alternative is a life dedicated to chasing
the ephemeral and transitory moments of ecstasy. When these
moments are concluded they become the starting point for new
desires. Those who would rule us for their own interests, from
the Roman emperors to the present, seek to enslave us to idols by
swallowing our emotional life up. They stage elaborate spectacles
and entertainment, filling us with a longing only they, like the
band, seem able to satiate.

Senturia, and those with her, embarked on a road toward spiritual obliteration, a road that led them away from life, a road that
led them toward nothingness, the final essence of death. They
saw the hypocrisy of a world infatuated with idols and worshipped another idol. The consequence was the same.

The world looks different when we strip away our comfort and security. In Roxbury we were ordinary men and women. The powerful and destructive forces of the ghetto were a daily reminder of our impotence and smallness. But many of those who taught theology at Harvard had a barely disguised disdain for the Bible and an inflated view of the role of their intellect in shaping the world. They assumed the right to speak on behalf of the poor and oppressed, although they knew nothing about them. The romantic images they conjured about the oppressed bore little correlation to the brutal life in the ghetto. The solutions they offered, using catch words such as "empowerment," were only possible if they kept themselves isolated and removed. The intrusion of reality on their illusions would, after all, obliterate them. They offered to us, to quote the lawyer William Stringfellow, who lived and worked in Harlem, little more than "poetic recitations . . . social analysis, gimmicks, solicitations, sentimentalities, and corn."[3]

Liberal theology, like its nemesis in the evangelical church, is a form of self-exaltation. While evangelicals often champion a gospel of greed and personal empowerment, deeply attractive to the poor and marginal, liberals often speak on behalf of oppressed groups they never meet, advocating utopian and unrealistic schemes to bring about peace and universal love. Neither group has much interest in testing their ideologies against reality.

The lectures I sat through in divinity school about oppression, liberation theology and the just-war theory were safely distant from the sordid realities we discussed. These discussions were an intellectual shell game, intriguing, even interesting, but finally meaningless without the visceral experience of the world.

The first time I saw a human being die in combat rendered hollow the platitudes about proper and improper uses of violence. I was no longer able to ask the question.

I was traveling north early one morning during the war in El Salvador on the Troncal highway to the Chalatenango province. Outside of the town of Aguilares I came upon several cars that had stopped before an open stretch of pavement. I heard intense bursts of gunfire up ahead, and then all went quiet.

I cautiously went forward by foot. When I neared the opening I saw a young soldier lying in the road with two dull black M-16s on either side of him. A few yards ahead, people were climbing onto an overcrowded bus.

The rebels had stopped the bus to collect "war taxes" when a pickup full of soldiers had sped past. The two groups had fired on each other. One soldier, who lay a few feet from me, had been shot through the back of the head. Another had been wounded. The truck had raced to the nearest army outpost and the rebels had disappeared in the bush. The bus driver, fearful of another clash, was shouting at his passengers to get back on board. The army would probably return soon and more fighting would follow.

I knelt down by the soldier, who could have been no more than 16. He was slowly curling himself into a fetal position. Blood came from his nose and the small bullet wound in the back of his head. A woman at the side of the road was watching in tears.

"Do you know him?" I asked.

She shook her head in the negative. I watched him die, far from his family and friends, an insignificant casualty in a war of "liberation."

What could any "new society," one many liberal Christians backed, ever mean to the family of this boy?

Can we really accept that 16-year-old soldiers, press-ganged into the military, are a regrettable sacrifice in the progression toward a new world or the Kingdom of God? I can accept his death as tragic and inevitable, given the social and historical antecedents leading up to the insurrection, but not as necessary. Idols, not God, require sacrifices. In his death I saw through the awful tragedy that is war, the inevitable sadness of it and the glib ways we can speak about experiences that are not our own.

Christian groups played an active role in supporting sides in the violent civil wars. I saw the hypocrisy of liberals and evangel-icals in Central America, each of whom chose sides and justified violence in the name of God. Pat Robertson traveled to camps in Honduras to support the contra bands, funded and backed by the United States, who were attacking Nicaragua. Many liberal reli-gious leaders embraced the Sandinista government or the Sal-vadoran rebels. To bless weapons and soldiers, something I once watched a Catholic bishop do at a military base in Guatemala, is to put faith in the idol of war, in the service of death. It is, per-haps, the most common and destructive form of idolatry, one that has left most religious institutions morally bankrupt.

The scene on the highway is seared in my consciousness. I see the bright, glaring sunlight. I see the boy dying on the road. I hear the rumbling of the diesel bus. I listen to the harried shouts of the driver. God was there, I know now, but not to bless either side. The tears of the sobbing woman were the tears of God.

Idols consume us. Only the small, mundane acts of life, of kindness for neighbors and friends and family, can save us. Moth-ers and fathers, who have put their own careers on hold, know this power, however hard it is to lose the identity and status that come with work. Those who stop to care for a sick or disabled relative know this. Sacrifice gives us life. It frees us from idols. But we must accept that such sacrifice can be hard and lonely. Sacrifice for others gives life and makes community possible. Sac-rifice for our idols leaves us with hollow, empty lives.

No institution or cause will remember or reward us for the sacrifices we make. There are no shortages of lives wrecked by idols. Those who spend their final years waiting forlornly for a call from children they never bothered to know because they were too busy building careers, must peer into the empty face of the idol they worshipped. Idols, when they finish with us, discard us. They keep us from God.

By checking out, by fleeing from concert to concert, by replacing real relationships with false relationships, ones built around the worship of an idol, the followers of the band descended into this moral and physical abyss. The disintegration swiftly became apparent. Some of the band's followers were reduced to poverty. They begged for food or spare change in the parking lots. They rarely bathed and often fell prey to drugs, always within easy reach. They become swallowed up by the obsession, an obsession that eventually saw crowds degenerate into unruly and hostile packs at some of the concerts.

"When you spend your teenage years living a life of lawless abandon, doing only what you want, you develop a sense of entitlement," Senturia said. "When you get enough of these people together, it can become dangerous."

What all who serve an idol fear is death, what Paul calls "the last enemy." It is the fear of eventual obliteration. It is the fear that death, like life, means nothing. It is a fear we rarely name but which hovers over us. The compulsiveness that drives us to consume too much, drink too much, take drugs or work too hard are bred from this fear of death, the fear that we will no longer exist, the fear that no matter what we do or say or accomplish our life will be meaningless, an insignificant blip on the screen.

Idols make us feel important. They make us feel, as long as we serve them, that we stand above the crowd. Our idols give us a larger identity, allowing us to define ourselves through the group. We are told we no longer need be insecure, uncertain and afraid. Our idols promise us the ability to rise above ourselves, to transcend time and place. Our idols tell us that nothing except ourselves and the group matter. Our idols tell us they can make us safe. And our idols, if we do not let go, lead to spiritual death, a life so devoid of meaning that only slavish devotion to the idol keeps us from having to face our caverns of emptiness.

Senturia said she had a difficult childhood. She wanted another childhood, one that did not hurt, one where she felt loved and appreciated. She found in the band "security, what seemed like unconditional love and what felt like a caring environment."

Her concert experiences were highly charged and overpowering.

"There are certain notes, certain moments in the music, where that may be the only way my body knows how to interpret whatever incredible feeling my mind is getting," she said.

She and others trailed the band for weeks as it moved from city to city. The time spent waiting for the next concert became excruciating, unbearable.

"I was addicted to a life where I had no responsibility," she said, "where everything was about the search for the next peak experience. It was narcissistic and hedonistic and ultimately empty. I had nothing to show for it afterward."

All other experiences in life began to pale, although the highs of the concert were harder and harder to replicate. The band toyed with emotions and would announce the mood they intended to create at a concert, saying that the show would be "dark" or "light."

"The band takes over a crowd," said Megan Leff, 28, who works in advertising in Manhattan. "They throw everyone into a fury. You cannot move or shake quickly enough. Then, suddenly, they will have everyone fall and pretend they are dead."

Senturia fled her demons, only to find that they arrived with her in each new city. She had to face them or allow her idol to destroy her life. The transitory highs only masked, for a moment, her pain. She had to stop and begin the hard task of living, forming real relationships and finding communities that did not worship idols.

"I would not be who I am today if I had not done this," Senturia said. "But I know now I am not going to find what I am looking for in parking lots in other cities. I will find what I am looking for only within myself. It is easier to get in a car and think that the next show will give you fulfillment. It is harder to sit in one place and confront life."

DECALOGUE III

LYING

You shall not take the name of the Lord your God in vain.

A cluster of women in tight jeans and halter tops wait for a turn at the phone at the Crystal Night Club in Hempstead, Long Island. They coo and whisper into the receiver as they lean into the bar. They talk of longing and of dreams, of being lonely and desiring company. They speak of love.

The night club, with its scattered tables, small dance floor and disco ball overhead is empty, save for thirty young women who had arrived a few minutes earlier in vans from Washington Heights in New York City. It is dimly lit and gloomy. I sit at the bar and listen to them speaking, trading the phone back and forth, their syrupy voices holding out in Spanish the tempting bait of affection. And to the men listening, seated in small apartment rooms with two or three other companions, far from wives and children, yearning for a soft touch, what is doled out is irresistible.

The women are not hookers. They make money on each drink a client buys for them. A plastic, fluted glass filled with ice and an ounce of cheap wine earns about $4 for the hostess and $6 for the house. Some women can earn $200 a night. The pretense of affection sells drinks. It is not an uncommon tactic; pick up any glossy magazine or switch on the television. We all want to be wanted, told we are attractive and desired, and if this comes in the form of a lie, however blatant and naked, the lie is often more appealing than facing the possibility of rejection.

Our consumer society is saturated with lies, the ones we are told, the ones we tell ourselves. And yet, having wandered through the bleak, soulless wastelands of communist East Germany, where all was gray and shoddy and tawdry, where the lies were so large and absurd they gave all conversations about life and politics an Alice-in-Wonderland quality, I always preferred returning to the neon-lit skyline and well-stocked stores in West Berlin. At least our lies come accompanied with a well-oiled sensual and emotional manipulation that in the rush of the moment allows our bodies to overpower our intellect. If I am going to be manipulated and lied to I prefer it be done with finesse. But all lies lead to despair. It is in our capacity to resist that we find worth, in our capacity to hold off the endless cycle of self-gratification, that we find what passes for happiness in human life.

There are whiskey bars like this around the world. They thrive on seedy back streets in port cities such as Athens, Buenos Aires and Marseilles, preying on the lonely. There are some 100,000 Salvadoran, Honduran and Guatemalan pot washers, construction workers or landscapers on Long Island, all living on the fringes of their communities, usually without their families. These are the patrons of the hostess bars, just as legions of male Chinese and East European immigrants patronized such establishments in other eras. The deafening blasts of music, gyrating women and booze-soaked conversations have been repeated other times in other tongues. It is an old scam. For a while, at least as long as they can pay, the men are wanted, needed and adored. And it is, if you have nothing else, better than the alternative.

A multiplicity of sexually alluring images assaults us. They flash in front of our eyes as we plod through our day. These images dangle another way of being in front of us, promising something better, although something we can never have. But we cherish the illusion. Life seems too bleak without it. We know, like these men, what is true and untrue, but we choose not to think, only to feel. In this we are no different from the men reeled in like fish.

Selsa Ortiz works her way through a list of numbers on a worn sheet of paper. She wears a floor-length black dress that has slits up to her hips and a rhinestone pin on the collar. Her face, heavily made up, is lit by the neon lights behind the counter. Her stomach, like that of many hostesses who must drink with their clients, presses out against the fabric. She is in her early thirties, but has a face that shows the wear of a woman who drinks too much and does not get enough sleep. We begin to speak.

"The bar keeps a list of who gets paychecks on Friday," she says between calls. "We have clients who are in love with us. They have no women except us. They come night after night until they cannot afford to come anymore. I have about ten regular clients. They are the ones who believe in love."

She has a red lollypop between her teeth. On her wrist is a gold bracelet. She turns in the middle of the conversation and casually picks up the phone, punching in a number from the piece of paper in front of her.

"Hello, Poppy," she says softly. "Are you alone tonight? I'm here. I am all alone. I miss you. I had a dream about you last night."

The men, their hands callused by rough work, begin to drift in through the door. The women greet their clients with smiles and usher them to tables. The sinewy frames of the laborers are packed into jeans and faded work shirts. They appear to know each other.

I walk to the top of the stairwell to escape the beat of the salsa music that throbs and pulsates throughout the room. Two men in jeans tromp up the wooden treads, past the neon-lit pool hall on the floor below. A bouncer frisks the men at the door, determines they do not have weapons and allows them inside. He tells me he confiscates dozens of knives and a few machetes hidden inside pant legs every night. He places a sticker on the confiscated weapons and gives another to the customer.

"They pick it up on the way home," he says, "which given these streets is not a bad idea."

When one man staggers toward him, drunk, he abruptly pushes him back down the stairs. The man reels, checks his balance against the wall, and turns to go, out into the cold winter slush, wandering on, I suspect, to another club.

They come like sheep. Most, I expect, know what will follow. They will be relieved here, or in some 20 other seedy dance clubs in the city, of their weekly pay. The obvious and open manipulation by the women is overpowered by the desperate thirst for affection, by the forlorn hope that, despite all the evidence, the affection is real. And perhaps this fiction of affection runs two ways, perhaps the girls, while finding the clients tedious and boring, also seek to imbue their work with meaning, with a belief that they provide comfort and warmth to those in need, that what they do is not duplicitous and cruel. The semblance of affection, of relationship, makes it easier for the manipulated and the manipulators, for the women who are sexual objects and the men who are objects of prey.

The immigrants in the bar cook food and wash dishes, clean houses, mow lawns, pick vegetables and gut and package chickens on poultry farms. They live among us yet are not of us. We do not translate compassion into our political life, assuming that individual acts of compassion and charity can compensate for injustice. The immigrants work without health insurance, workers' compensation, union protection, unemployment benefits, legal recourse or retirement benefits. They live in fear of being picked up and deported. Once arrested they disappear for weeks, or months, shuttled between county jails, sometimes hundreds of miles from where they live in states like Louisiana or Texas. They are not provided with legal representation. Their cases do not appear on the public docket. All hearings are closed and judges will not confirm or deny if the cases exist. They are treated as nonpersons, until they are shackled, crammed into a van, driven to an airport and deported, sometimes to a country they have not seen in years.

I watch the curious rituals of false courtship. The well-choreographed dance is familiar, the careful counterfeiting of love. We all want to be loved, to be needed. We turn, when lonely, also to charlatans who soothe us, who tell us we are valuable and important, but who regard us in the paneled warrens of their spacious offices as pawns to move on a chess board. The television evangelists have tapped into this burning need. God will bless us, shower us with wealth and success, as long as we mail in the checks. We are used and eventually discarded by the institutions where we work. They manipulate us for their own gain, holding out the promise of status, respect and love. They create false communities, ones that strive to push us to identify with the goals and prestige of the corporation or the nation or the church. It is not unconditional love. It is very conditional love. When we fail to please the god of production and profit, when we fall afoul of the rigid codes of behavior imposed upon us, when we question dogma or rules, when we denounce injustices, we are thrust into exile, tossed out like the men who arrive at the door of the club drunk and unsteady.

Sympathy and understanding is possible on an individual level. It is not possible from an institution, although human resources departments work hard to delude us, even referring to the company as a family. The goal of every institution is its own perpetuation. Those who are loyal to individuals, who place individuals above profit, do not last long. For when the institution is in trouble, as anyone who has been laid off from work knows, it is we who are sacrificed. It is hard and painful to accept that we are not vital, that those we work for care little about us, that we are expendable. We need the lies, need them to keep going, need them so we can miss the school plays and baseball games, all the little markers in the lives of our children, who really do love us, although not as we always want to be loved and not always in ways that exalt us.

We are desperate to inflate our worth. The lies told by bosses in suits are no less pernicious than the lies told by these bar girls. They are the same lies: you are valued, you are loved, you are wanted. They are the lies we pay money to hear, the lies that fuel the vast advertising industry, the engine of our consumer society, the lies peddled by those who use patriotism to send our children to wars that should never be fought. And those who are most susceptible to the lies are those who have the least power, for they hunger to be included.

We are no different from these men. We may, like these bar patrons, acknowledge the manipulation; certainly we are all aware of how we are manipulated as consumers, but in the end we cannot accept that the cold forces that cajole and seduce us, that inflate our self-worth, care nothing for us. This is too emotionally devastating to our image of ourselves, an image created in large part by those who use us.

Many of these men in the bar are from El Salvador. They fought or lived through the war I covered for five years. One man, too drunk to be allowed into the club, stands on the curb outside. We remember specific engagements and commanders. We talk about the rebels and their clandestine radio station. We pass back and forth the concrete names of villages and rivers, of mountains and roads, of weapons, in short all the hard details that, to those who have been there, conjure up a war.

"I was in the Atlacatl Battalion," he says, naming an elite battalion that carried out numerous atrocities. "I was a sergeant in the Atlacatl for five years."

I ask him if he was in the battalion in 1981. He nods. On December 10 of that year, in the village of El Mozote in the province of Morazán, units from the battalion rounded up all the men, women and children. They locked them in their houses and the next day began to execute them in groups, many of the men first being tortured. The final groups formed for execution were children. By the time the soldiers were done over 500 people from El Mozote and surrounding villages lay dead. The massacre was denied by the Salvadoran government and the U.S. Embassy, which claimed falsely that it had investigated what took place.

It is clear from my question that the deeds of the battalion are known to me. We stand in silence. He leans against the large window of a pizza parlor. His work boots are soaked from the dirty slush. The wind whips down the empty street. He begins to cry, his chest heaving up and down, thin tears running down his cheeks, the air coming in and out of his lungs with raspy gulps. I wonder what demons are circling in his head, what cries of anguish he carries with him from the humidity and heat of a Salvadoran province to this frigid, lonely street corner in Long Island. I wonder if this is why he drinks. I pity him, but for the sake of the dead I hope he will never forget.

War entails the greatest deception, the greatest lie. Leaders must convince people to face death, all the while promoting the fiction that they are also willing to sacrifice themselves. The leaders have no intention of making any sacrifice. Their own children do not go to war. They use secrecy to foster an aura of mystery and invincibility, to hide the huge profits made by defense corporations and the falsehoods told to make us fight, the savage barbarity of war itself. They tell us we are noble, powerful, that self-sacrifice in war, the ultimate sacrifice, will turn us into heroes who will be honored by the grateful nation. They paint service to the nation as the highest moral act we can commit. They want us to confuse physical courage with moral courage. But as war grinds on, as more and more bodies are needed to fuel the conflict, it becomes a cold, impersonal enterprise. The secrecy grows. The lies get bigger and bigger.

Elias Canetti in *Crowds and Power* writes:

Anyone who wants to rule men first tries to humiliate them, to trick them out of their rights and their capacity for resistance, until they are as powerless before him as animals. He uses them like animals and, even if he does not tell them so, in himself he always knows quite clearly that they mean just as little to him; when he speaks to his intimates he will call them sheep or cattle. His ultimate aim is to incorporate them into himself and to suck the substance out of them. What remains of them afterwards does not matter to him. The worse he has treated them, the more he despises them. When they are no more use at all, he disposes of them as he does of his excrement, simply seeing to it that they do not poison the air of his house.[1]

Faced with the truth of our own powerlessness, our own insignificance, our own manipulation, we would, like this immigrant, collapse. We cannot face the rawness of our manipulation, glossing it over with the myth. It is easier to pretend.

Lies swirl around us, spinning complex webs of meaning that delude the great and the small, the manipulated and the manipulators. The streets around the night club stink of them. There are storefront offices where self-appointed immigration specialists with phony credentials prey on the desperate. They bleed them dry of huge sums of cash, promising to secure them a green card or halt deportation proceedings. The less power people have, the more these vultures congregate to feed off the weak and desperate.

We are consumers of lies, lies pumped out over the airwaves, lies that promise that if we spend more money, if we buy this brand or that product, we will be respected, envied, powerful, loved. It never works, but rather than face the truth we turn back to those who seduce us, who draw us into their embrace, who tell us what we want to hear. We beg them for more. We return night after night to our own glittery clubs where we ingest lies until our money runs out. And when we fall into despair we medicate ourselves, as if there is something wrong with us, not with the world around us, as if the happiness we have failed to find in the hollowness of the deceptive game is part of our deficiency. And, of course, we are told it is.

The men in the bar do not expect much from the night. The outings always have the same conclusion. The women disappear shortly before dawn, being driven home in the vans. They leave their dates bereft, often drunk and alone.

The women, who can dart between two or three men at once, have spindly legs and bulging stomachs. Alcoholics make the best employees. I watch the owner, Luis Tejada, bark orders at girls from behind the bar.

"Girls in these bars like to drink, that is what it boils down to," Tejada, who like most club owners is Dominican, tells me. "Some of these women can drink these guys to the floor. I have girls that can down sixty-five glasses in a night. That is the record. The average is fifty on a Saturday night."

The stairway leading up to the club stinks of urine by the end of the night. When I walk outside to the stairwell to escape the noise, the smoke and the crowd, I see two men collapsed on the steps in alcoholic stupors. Vomit lies near the face of one of the men. I wonder if they have someone, somewhere, who loves them, some woman back home in El Salvador or Guatemala, maybe a couple of kids, who wait for their daddy. They deserve more than this.

Ivan Escalante, 24, is thin, with dark black hair. He is from El Salvador and has worked for five years as a pot washer. He, like most of these men, lacks proper documents and cannot open a bank account. He shares a $400-a-month room with two other men and sends $150 weekly to his family. Payday, for him and many others, is the hardest day of the week. It is then that the women call him from the bars.

"We live a life for others, for those at home," he tells me. "We have no lives here. As soon as we are paid we become vulnerable. We cannot keep money in our room, someone will steal it. None of us have cars, so we must walk. And on the streets of Hempstead there are a lot of assaults from the Salvadoran street gangs. The only distractions we have are the bars, but once you get here it is hard to stop. The cash is in your pocket. It is nice to talk and dance with a woman."

The women who cajole the money from their customers know the income is intended for families, families that need it for food and clothing, families that put up with the misery of having their men here because they are poor. This is how they survive.

"When you wake up and realize your money is gone, that it has been wasted on girls and drinks, you are depressed," Juan Antonio Hernandez, a Salvadoran dishwasher who works in Bayville, tells me. "You know your children in El Salvador will not get enough to eat this week. It is horrible."

The streets, when workers reel drunkenly home to the overcrowded apartments, are also fraught with predators. Young men belonging to Salvadoran street gangs in Long Island such as the Mara Salvatrucha or MS-13 gather on corners near the clubs or sit sullenly in the backs of clubs nursing beers, avoiding the women and looking for easy targets. There are two gang members in the bar this night, vultures with greasy hair and black leather jackets. They sit at a table on the far end of the room with their backs to the wall.

Tejada refills fluted glasses, collects bills and puts a mark on a yellow pad next to the name of each woman who asks him for a drink. A large wad of bills is in his left hand. The roar of the music, a Puerto Rican pop song, makes communication difficult. He and his hostesses shout.

"This is where men come for the concept of having a girlfriend," he explains loudly over the bar. "All the bars in Hempstead have dancing waitresses. They dance, sit and converse with you as long as you buy them drinks. The men fall in love with the girls. This brings them back night after night. Every once in a while one of the girls elopes with a customer, but once that happens they are out of a job.

"When a customer finds out he cannot get a girl, he will leave for a few weeks," he adds. "But he will usually come back and try with another. I go for the drinks, not what the girls look like. I have some Petunia Pigs that drink a lot more and are worth more to me than the Christie Brinkleys. This is strictly about money. Besides, these guys are not Tom Cruise."

Juana Franco is 29 and has five children. She studies at Bronx Community College. She stands outside the door at the top of the stairwell smoking a cigarette during a break. She watches as a drunk weaves his way unsteadily down the stairs, his back to us, his feet landing with difficulty on the treads. He gets to the bottom, lurches off a wall and then pushes open the front door.

"You don't have to sit with someone like that," she says acidly. "When you see that they are really drunk, you go the other way."

She moves aside to allow a group of men to pass her into the club. They leer at her tight blue spandex pants. She has a look of supreme indifference on her face. She takes another drag on her cigarette.

"They all say they are single," she says, "even when they are married. No one put a gun to their heads to make them come here, but still you feel sorry for them. We all have feelings."

The police say they haven't found any evidence of prostitutes in the bars, and owners say that women who sleep with customers or use drugs are fired. But if the men want a prostitute they can go to one of the brothels in apartments in the town where the rooms are broken up into little plywood cubicles. In each cubicle is a mattress, a box of condoms, and a girl. Clients get ten minutes for twenty dollars.

These encounters are not ones where there is any semblance of affection or communication. They are brief, physical bursts and rapid animal-like retreats. The men say they leave feeling lonely, anxious to escape the cubicles as if fleeing a crime.

"If they sleep with a customer I lose clients," says Tejada, who tells me he has made enough on his business to retire. "They won't spend money to buy her drinks if they get what they want. I only make money while they are trying to get her. Why buy a cow when you get the milk?

"The women have to be focused," he says. "They have to be disciplined."

These lies, the ones told in the bar, the ones told to us, create false communities. They weaken and destroy real communities. These false communities, which we must pay to enter, are a way to fight despair. We share this despair with these men. We share it with almost everyone around us, although we work hard to pretend it does not exist, this despair of living and dying, of not being the person we want to be, or what we want people to believe we are.

> Faces along the bar
> Cling to their average day:
> The lights must never go out,
> The music must always play,
> All the conventions conspire
> To make this fort assume
> The furniture of home;
> Lest we should see where we are,
> Lost in a haunted wood,
> Children afraid of the night
> Who have never been happy or good. [2]

Revenge takes place in the bathroom. There the men, often drunk and aware that they must soon stagger home alone, turn on the porcelain fixtures. The rage, checked and muted most of the time, erupts. It is the self-destruction I saw in the ghetto, the self-destruction of those who know no other way of fighting back, but to tear down their own life, the one they hate, the one they blame themselves for not being able to escape. This rage is the consequence of living in a world where we are manipulators and manipulated, where we beg to be fed the lies to mask the loneliness.

"They destroy everything that is not nailed down," Tejada says. "I have to remodel the bathroom every month because the toilets, sinks and urinals get ripped out. I am looking into stainless steel fixtures, like the ones in jails. The men are frustrated. They spend all their money on girls and get nothing in return. They take it out on my bathroom. It is the only place they ever have privacy."

THE SABBATH

Remember the sabbath day, to keep it holy.

At the age of ten, after being given an academic scholarship, I was packed off to a boarding school in Massachusetts. The school was perched on a hill. There was a pond in the center of the campus where we skated in winter and waded around barefoot in the muck catching frogs in the spring. A bell on a post next to the pond was rung for meals. There was a glass and brick school house, known as the learning center, brick dormitories, a gym, an arts studio, a huge wooden lodge that served as the dining hall and athletic fields. We went to school six days a week, were herded into the assembly area at night, known as the pit, to do homework and were given, perhaps, an hour of free time a day.

We lived under the glare of tyrannical teachers, known as masters. Life was regimented. We wore white shirts with our blue-and-red-striped school ties, gray flannel slacks, a blue school blazer with the school emblem on the breast pocket, black lace shoes and black socks. Our dress code rarely varied. In the heat of late spring we could wear a seersucker suit coat. We all had one black suit. The black suit was worn on the Sabbath.

My first two years in boarding school I lived in a cubicle, a narrow enclosure with walls that did not reach the ceiling. It had a bed, chair, one window and a radiator under the window. Our cubicles lay in two long rows with a hallway down the middle. At the end of the hallway, at the top of the stairs leading to the bathroom, lived our master, Mr. Richards. The cubicles had a closet and a bureau built into the wall. When we studied we pulled out a board from the middle of the bureau and sat on the bed. There was a curtain on a rod so that we could close off the room, but it was a collective life.

Mr. Richards was tall, wiry and unapproachable. He carried a small metal box that held his collection of items found in the dining hall food. Our chief pleasure was to torment him. We stole spoons from the dining hall and when lights were turned out at 9:30 we began to bang on the radiators until the pipes vibrated and clanged. Mr. Richards's door burst open. The lights would be flicked on. We would be threatened with a collective punishment, like detention, or loss of the Saturday night movie, and then it would go dark again and his door would slam shut. Soon, often enough, the racket would begin again. We spent many weeks paying for our resistance.

I do not know if Mr. Richards, or anyone who ran the school, was particularly religious, but it was assumed that religion was a good thing, at least the formal adherence to religious ritual and doctrine. Religion, like learning, was part of the effort to bend us into dutiful and compliant young men. It was meant to curb any thoughts of rebellion, of self-expression, of liberation. Mr. Richards decided that every night we would take turns reading one of the Psalms. This began well enough, Mr. Richards's Bible being handed to a boy in his pajamas who read a selection, shut the book and then climbed into bed for lights-out. But it soon came to our attention that the 119th Psalm ran on for a few pages. If we read it slowly we could ward off lights-out for ten, sometimes fifteen minutes. This lasted a few nights until Mr. Richards announced we were only allowed to read the much shorter 23rd Psalm.

We functioned, insofar as those who governed the school could make us, as a captive herd. We were contained by schedules, rules, demands, mountains of homework, dining hall chores and compulsory athletics. Hazing was endemic, with older boys taking out the frustrations and anger, a life with little love or affection, on the smaller ones. Complaining was useless, not only because masters, who talked a lot about making us into men, looked at those who complained as whiners, but because the retribution was sure to be worse than what we had endured. The hazing created a kind of hierarchy of the strong, with boys on the lower end of the rung trying desperately to divert abuse by turning on those who were weaker and more vulnerable. Those who were small or odd or different or overly sensitive had the hardest time.

To boys who did not have the verbal dexterity to belittle tormentors or the ability to fight back, life was bleak. There was a boy in our cubicles who flailed his belt against his wall at night and cried, "Mommy! Mommy! Mommy!" There was another, nicknamed "the phantom pooper," who defecated with regularity in his pants. A boy who was a dwarf suffered the most. His various deformities, including poor eyesight and thick glasses and a slight curvature of his spine, saw him taunted mercilessly. I wonder what his parents could have been thinking when they sent him away. I developed an acidic tongue and a willingness to fight, even against those larger than myself. To fail to stand up to bullies was an invitation to perpetual misery. But there was a cost. Teeth were chipped and broken. Bruises were common. I once ended up in the hospital with internal bleeding after being repeatedly kicked by another boy.

Favored boys were awarded little round lapel pins with different-colored eagles in public assemblies at the end of each trimester. These red, blue, silver or gold eagles denoted more than good grades, for there were semesters I made the dean's list but did not receive an eagle. They denoted "citizenship" or in short, doing what you were told. Those who received nothing were, in our slang, awarded "black vultures." The effect of not getting an eagle was devastating. As a small boy, denied an eagle, I cloistered myself in one of the piano practice rooms after the ceremony and sobbed in disgrace. Our parents knew of us only through the filter of the school. Bad reports never reflected on the school, but on those of us who desperately longed for approval from parents we saw only a few times a year.

We were fed generous doses of social snobbery, told that we attended the best school in the country and that we were being molded into leaders. I remember few actual assemblies, but I remember the one about the importance of becoming "Renaissance men," men able to excel in the arts, science and athletics. One quick look around the assembly at the slouching, bored gathering of pimpled and vacant boys, most of whom attended the school because their parents were wealthy, gave the talk a discernible ridiculousness. There were long windy talks about what it took to be a man, filled with the usual clichés. Intellectual independence, and with it the spirit of self-criticism, was ruthlessly crushed. Those who succeeded were those who obeyed, believed what they were told and assisted the authoritarians above us in maintaining order. Initiative and originality were threatening to the school, which like most schools, was designed to promote mediocrity.

The world radiated outward from our little school. The masters appeared to hold the fate of our lives in their hands, wielding an Olympian power that would forever color our existence. Black marks on our record or expulsion, we were told, would be irrevocably damaging to our future. We believed this. We were young. We had no mother and father to go home to at night, no one to tell us otherwise. All love, if one can call the giving or withholding of praise by the school administrators love, was conditional. When we failed it seemed as if an awful dark pit yawned before us and threatened to engulf us in perpetual shame. Being called before a master for some infraction, even a minor one, saw our rulers speak in apocalyptic words about our fate. The technique was effective. We were a cowed and miserable group.

The hypocrisy of the school was not lost on most of us, although we believed a lot more of the cant than we should have. As in all male boarding schools there were pedophiles, single men who desired to live in close proximity to young boys. The master of my dorm when I was 13 frequently invited a classmate into his apartment, located at the end of the hallway. He had set up a black light with posters and pillows in a small room. The boy would go in and the door would lock. I rarely saw my classmate come out. We returned from Christmas break to find that the master and the boy were no longer at school, although the reasons for the sudden departure were never explained.

There was an *Animal Farm* quality to the flowery rhetoric about our budding nobility and success, along with the references to the school's warm nurturing environment. And yet, it was easier emotionally to ignore the sad truth for the fantasy, to believe that we were fated to lead great lives, that the school was the finest in the nation and that the masters, whose behavior should have tipped us off, cared for us and would mold us into exceptional leaders. By the time I left, five years later, I had a deep hostility to authority and a visceral distaste for the snobbery of the "well born."

I remember only one act of rebellion. It took place after lunch one fall afternoon before the winter snows. The headmaster announced after lunch, for each meal was followed by announcements, that all boys would walk down to the base of the hill leading up to the dining hall. We were ordered to stand in a line and walk slowly up the hill collecting rocks so the slope would be clear for mowing. The headmaster, and several of the teachers, stood at the top of the hill. We advanced slowly, stooping down to put rocks in our pockets, complaining to our neighbors. And then one boy stood and hurled a rock toward the teachers above us. Another boy hurled his rocks. Soon the whole school was throwing stones at the retreating teachers. By the time we got to the top we were breathless with excitement and fear. They could hardly punish all of us, and indeed they did not, although they punished the older boys who led the assault. Incidents such as this one, like the quietly dismissed pedophiles, were never referred to in public.

The teachers and administrators were the guardians of our future. Certainly some had honorable motives, I remember a few with affection, but in the climate of manipulation and severe restrictions, most of us spent our boyhood in a cruel and bizarre universe. I had no idea how much I detested my years there until I returned two decades later to speak. As the car climbed the hill, one I had often walked up and down, my stomach wound itself in a knot of anxiety and loathing. I wanted to flee. All the buried emotions of my boyhood were unleashed.

On Sunday mornings, dreading what was to come, we all appeared in the dining hall in our black suits. Sundays were the Sabbath. We ate breakfast at our assigned tables and lined up by form, or grade, to walk down the hill on which the school was perched. We were required to carry our school checkbooks so we could place a check in the collection plate. We escaped for some weeks this drain on our meager finances, since amounts in our bank accounts were limited by the school, by dropping IOU's into the plate. This practice, like every attempt at defiance, was soon forbidden.

The 180 boys set off each Sunday down the hill. On cold days we all wore identical black overcoats. We passed the few houses, the cemetery, went under an arched stone railroad bridge, past a farm with its pungent smell of cow manure and into the town with its historic homes. We filed reluctantly into the church and sat together in the wooden box pews with latch doors. The minister's wife, who was amply endowed, played the organ at the back of the church. It was rumored that she had been Miss Texas. Most of us spent the service with our heads turned toward the organ loft.

The words in the sermons of compassion and love, of sin and forgiveness, of redemption, of resurrection, were abstractions that bore no relationship to our harsh reality. The hymns were turgid, the creeds and recitations boring and the sermons never challenging us to question the idols of success and elitism, the idols held up by those who had us in their grip. We went through the ritual of church the same way we went through all school rituals. Church was one more pillar in the scaffolding being erected around us. It was meant to circumscribe our actions. Religion was irrelevant to us. It bore no relationship to our world, indeed our world rarely impinged on the service.

There were no structured activities, a rarity in our life, on Sundays. But the Sabbath was a day of deep depression. I am not sure we could articulate it, but we knew we were missing something, something important, a home, affection, warmth, and a mother and father who cared about us. These were the loneliest moments of my childhood. A black mood settled on the campus. My enduring memory of the Sabbath is of a bleak, gray November afternoon, although there must have been sunlit days. It was the worst moment of the week. We waited only for the day to end, the night to pass and school to begin on Monday.

I see now that we never celebrated the Sabbath. The Sabbath is about honoring those we love and those who love us, honoring the essence of the divine. By turning away from work, from the world, to cherish those we love, we honor the Sabbath. The Sabbath is not about one day. It is about taking time for a daughter's basketball game, a son's track race, a dinner where a family talks. The Sabbath is a moment when a couple sits on a bench and reaffirms love. The Sabbath is the time set aside to nurture all that gives us meaning in life, all that makes life worth living. The Sabbath is the recognition that work, that all the hours we spend making a living, are in fact the means to this end, to the ability to have and sustain love. When we ignore the Sabbath we destroy that which we should be working to achieve.

Institutional religion has often attempted to confine the Sabbath to the idol of the physical church, the synagogue or the mosque, to restrict its celebration to within its walls. It has sought to make the act of worship holy, limited and contained in a space and time, without understanding that the Sabbath is a way of being. And in this it has divorced the Sabbath from the reality of daily life, from the need to love and be loved. Sabbath rituals, as in my boarding school, become in the hands of the institutions sterile and empty, mocking the purpose of the day.

Honoring the Sabbath is one of the most important of the commandments. It occupies a third of the text of the commandments. Our restless lives cry out for the peace of the Sabbath. The Sabbath is the culmination of our life, the moment when we pay homage to forces of creation. And if we are unable to experience this spiritual transcendence, if we are cut off from love, as we were as boys, then our spiritual and moral life shrivels and decays. The Sabbath was the darkest day of the week for us because it was a reminder of what we were denied.

In the commandments the word "holy" is applied to only one word, the "Sabbath." The Sabbath is not about being in a particular place at a particular time. It is about honoring relationships. It is not about male or female, husband or wife, children or parents, at least not exclusively; it is about the power of love to transform us. To ignore the Sabbath is to deny the source of life.

The rituals we carry out during the Sabbath connect us to those who, performing much the same ritual, have honored in the past the transforming power of love. It is a way of tying us to the greater community of humankind, the generations lost in the dust of time, those who passed their love on to us. The Sabbath calls us away from the lies and temptations used to empower us so we can give of ourselves to empower others.

"Suppression of a desire is considered a sacrilege that must inevitably avenge itself in the form of some mental disorder," Rabbi Abraham Heschel wrote. "We worship not one but a whole pantheon of needs and have come to look upon moral and spiritual norms as nothing but personal desires in disguise."[1]

The Sabbath is the battle for transcendence, for freedom from the pull of "needs." It is the battle for life. It is the battle to defeat that which destroys love, the idolatry of desire, the hard and concrete cases of injustice, all that belittles the worth of other human beings. The boarding school held before us idols. It spurred us forward to meet their demands. Religion was about abstractions that killed the vitality and passion of faith. Religion was never allowed to get in the way of the demands made by the idols of success and power.

The prophets spent their days raging against corruption and abuse of power by those in the royal palaces and courts, the mistreatment of the poor, of widows and orphans, in short the hard and difficult struggle by the oppressed to achieve freedom and dignity. They were angry, indignant over minor infractions. The prophets, I understood years later, would have been standing on the bottom of the hill with us, not at the top with the school officials who ruled us. But the message of the prophets, like all messages passed to us, was twisted to pressure us to conform.

The Sabbath is not about rules. These are imposed by institutions which seek conformity and control. Religious authorities in the wars I covered willingly put their institutions in the service of nationalist or ethnic violence. They legitimized the abuse and murder of others outside the faith. They sanctified war. They turned their religious texts into venomous calls for death and vengeance. Christians, Jews and Muslims were indistinguishable in championing ruthless crusades in the name of their faith. This was as true in the Middle East as in the Balkans. Many faiths turned the Sabbath into a ceremony used to nurture hatred and revenge, mocking the essence of the commandment. Conformity to order and ritual, a dangerous self-worship, took the place of honoring the Sabbath.

Those who honor the Sabbath must often do it surreptitiously. To honor the Sabbath, in a way that is meaningful, is to often defy religious authorities. It requires us to break rules rather than enforce them, to be inclusive where we are told to exclude. There are those who honor the Sabbath without naming it. There are those who honor it in a catacomb religion, one where orthodoxy is replaced by authenticity. Honoring the Sabbath often means defying the attempts of religious institutions to define it.

The Nos. 1 and 9 trains rumble past every few minutes, shaking the windows on the 20th-floor apartment in Morningside Heights in New York. The screeches and throaty rattle of the subway cars drown out the conversation. And when no lines of trains were pumping along the elevated track, car alarms, sirens and trucks squealed—the intrusive noises, in short, of Manhattan.

"There are nights I wake up and think I am sleeping on the subway platform," says Stephen Arpadi, a pediatrician who has spent his career taking care of children with HIV.

Steve, bearded and casually dressed, moves through his small apartment lined with books on medicine and Jewish theology. His wife, Terry Marx, also a pediatrician—they met in medical school—mixes two vodka gimlets.

On Friday nights, the start of the Jewish Sabbath, they engage in their ritual of mixed drinks and the practice of allowing their two daughters to watch a video, or what they call "Shabbat TV." Their interpretation of the ritual of keeping the Sabbath holy is not only part of their effort to reconcile the demands of modernity and faith, but also to retain a spiritual core.

"I suppose some traditionalists would be appalled at our lack of adherence to the letter of the laws of Shabbat," Terry says. "Shabbat TV is, of course, an oxymoron. Shabbat candles are supposed to be lit eighteen minutes before sundown, not when everything is ready. Television and cooking are prohibited once Shabbat begins. Gimlets are not even on the radar screen. But these are our rituals. They are part of our struggle to honor if not the letter of Shabbat then the spirit of Shabbat."

In the next room their daughters, Charlotte and Adina, sit around the glow of the television. The parents cook dinner, talk in low voices and prepare the table.

"I grew up in Detroit with the worst of American Judaism," Terry says. "Meaning was defined by socializing. There was a total lack of spirituality. After high school I had nothing to do with the Jewish community."

Their work as pediatricians made it harder and harder to slip into weekends devoted to entertainment. They saw too much. They thought too much. They began to search. They did not come out of strong religious backgrounds, although Steve's father fled Berlin shortly before World War II. They drifted as young doctors to alternative religious gatherings and congregations, some where participants led their own services and a rabbi was not present.

"During my medical training I began to be drawn to more organized Jewish religious life," he says. "I needed a place where I could go after what I saw in the hospital. I needed to contemplate things beyond the here and now, beyond the material world. A lot happens in my waking hours as a doctor. I see bad things happen to people. I think a lot about the human condition. You can go to therapy to deal with some of this, but therapy can only help you find out who you are. It cannot answer why I am here."

The couple began to attend an Upper West Side synagogue, which, at the time, was run by Rabbi Marshal T. Meyer. They started to meet their Jewish friends there on Friday nights. It became a pattern they would not break.

"I guess, although at the time we were not conscious of it, this was when we began as a couple to mark the Sabbath," Terry says.

And then her grandfather, who had emigrated from Russia, died. She flew back to Detroit for the funeral and sat in his home sitting Shiva. No one in her family, however, could say Kaddish, the Jewish prayer for the dead. She took the book and began, haltingly, stumbling and often unsure of the pronunciation of some words.

"I felt like a ridiculous imposter," she says, "and I realized that the death of my grandfather meant in our family the death of tradition."

The experience pushed her to put her daughters in a Jewish day school. As they nurtured their two young girls, the AIDS epidemic began to claim the lives of Steve's patients. He found himself standing by bedsides with distraught parents or grandparents as his patients died. The world outside began to seem, at times, trivial. Life, he understood, could be swift—too swift—and callous. He had to "reconcile that awful things happen with this notion of a God."

"I have spent a lot of time thinking about death," he says. "It is up close and personal. This is part of my determination to honor Shabbat. Life is really a blink. We are all very, very vulnerable. I want to live a more mindful life. I feel power in the presence of these kids whose lives have just ended. It drives home our finiteness.

"It shows me how life is not really so concrete or tangible. These children are a presence for me."

The older children who knew they are dying often asked the same questions: "Will I die alone?" and "Will I be alone when I am dead?"

"Many children whose parents died of AIDS are told by other family members that they will soon be with their mother or father," he says. "They find comfort in this. Even if it is a fiction, it is a good fiction."

Death, like life, rose above him in its mystery. He accepted that there would always be things in life beyond his ability to understand, yet things he felt he should honor.

"I have to believe that God suffers when bad things happen to these kids," he says. "Whatever God's majesty and power, God does not prevent pediatric AIDS. Maybe that is where we as doctors come in."

It is dark. The Shabbat dinner, for those who follow Jewish law to the letter, should have begun. But the dinner was not ready when the sun went down. The movie is not over. The parents want to talk.

"I struggle with belief," Terry says. "I do not know if God exists. I go to synagogue. I hold Shabbat, but I have doubts. I just decided to put them on the back burner and go on."

The family gathers around the plates of chicken, salad and baked potatoes. Terry lights the candles. Steve gives the blessing over the wine. The couple bless the children. They break the bread and eat.

The girls, unlike their parents, are fluent in Hebrew. They attend the Abraham Heschel School on the Upper West Side. Jewish thought and history are part of the curriculum. They have grown up differently.

"We do not want to make religious ritual oppressive," Terry says. "We want to come together as a family after we have been atomized for the week. There is a counterculture quality to this moment. Shabbat is the antidote to popular culture. It is designed to make you think, to fight the forces of materialism, selfishness, acquisition, competitiveness, self-gratification and entitlement. Maybe there are other ways to carry on this struggle. I am not a Buddhist. I do not meditate. We do it through Judaism."

Whatever happens in the lives of their daughters, whether they embrace faith or not, one thing is certain: the girls, when the day comes, will be able to recite, as fluently as their grandfather, the Kaddish.

THE FAMILY

Honor your father and your mother.

My father was singularly unfit for the U.S. Army. When he spoke about his experience as an army sergeant in World War II in North Africa you could almost see him push his rifle away. He disdained all talk of heroics in war, abhorred the glorification of battle and steered us away from the ordered display of weapons in museums, reminding us that these were machines designed to kill human beings.

I am not sure he ever went so far as to declare himself a pacifist, but he was a pacifist by nature. I could not picture him shooting a person, something as a cryptographer he fortunately never had to do. He had an innate kindness and decency, a deep sensitivity, which protected him from the intoxication of war and violence.

The stories he told us from the war were not ones that made you want to rush down to the recruiting office. He talked about sleeping in cold mud and being punished for not keeping the barrel of his weapon clean, of the deadening boredom of army life and especially guard duty, of the discomfort of life in the desert, of how, because of infections caused by the sand, most of his unit had to be marched back to be swiftly circumcised in an army medical tent. He talked about the stupidity of officers and the even greater stupidity of the military machine that devoured human lives. The only time he fired his rifle at a living object came when he and some friends hunted a gazelle. As he talked about the animal, running wounded as he and the others pumped rounds at it until its guts fell out, his voice would crack. He described its stomach falling out before it collapsed in a heap. He could not bring himself to eat it.

He went to the University of Missouri after the war to be a newspaper reporter, thought better of it, went on to seminary and became a Presbyterian minister. He spent his life in the parish ministry, but the war, and with it a deep distrust of all authority, permeated the rest of his life. He never joined the activities of the veterans in the VFW Hall, a place where men gathered in our small town mostly to drink. The hall, like the dimly lit Glass Bar on Main Street, had the aura of an opium den, especially for those of us living in a manse where there was no alcohol.

I grew up, until boarding school intervened, in a farm town in upstate New York. We lived in a large white clapboard house that was next to the red brick church. My mother taught school in the next town. The house, built in 1801, was drafty and creaky, but the rooms were large. In the winter my sister and I sat on the iron grille vents when the furnace shot up bursts of warm air. My room, with its wide pine floorboards, looked out on Main Street. I sat at the window and watched the life of the town. I loved the stories, the array of characters, including the cranky and often inebriated caretaker of the cemetery: a retarded man who rumor had it had been rendered an imbecile after suffering from a mustard gas attack in World War I; and the odd eccentrics, including the old German submariner from World War I who lived in a shack in the woods behind our house and kept his Iron Cross in a wooden box. An isolated community of poor whites, known as Sloughters, probably with a mixture of black and Indian blood, lived in poverty on Spring Street, as well as in enclaves outside of town. They were the pariahs of the village.

The Sloughters were rumored to be the products of incestuous relationships, given to drink and driftlessness. But my father had a special warmth for them. They often showed up at his office. There was no social worker in town, no one to take their side, and my father's view of authority probably coincided with their own. The high school principal had a habit of throwing unruly Sloughter kids out of school and my father, despite his mild temperament, fought with the man to get the children back into school. The principal finally threatened to get a restraining order to keep my father off the school grounds. It was a running battle, one that contributed to my going away to school and my sister finishing her schooling in the next town.

The town I knew in my childhood has vanished. The characters who loomed large in my youth are gone. I found many of them in the cemetery, the headstones with the names of the elderly widows who helped me with my stamp and coin collection, my dentist and neighbors. I walked past the rows of headstones. Their faces floated in front of me. The town below the cemetery seemed a shell, all the life, or at least the life I knew, sucked out of it. Those who remained seemed smaller, as if time had shrunk them to mortal size. The town's stone courthouse, the manse, the church with its gleaming steeple seemed strange and distantly familiar.

My first short stories and poems, done with the encouragement of my mother, who made them into a little book, were about what I saw, or rather imagined went on behind the facade. I knew enough to grasp that appearances masked another reality, one that was not as decent and upright as it looked from the outside. I kept a bulky collection of fossils in wooden crates against the wall. My father drove me to farms where I searched the rocks in the meandering stone walls for fossilized trilobites, fish and crinoid stems. I had a large collection of arrowheads given to me by the farmers who unearthed them in their fields.

My father's office was in a low, whitewashed single-story building behind the church. It had a red leather swivel chair and a print by Salvador Dali of Christ nailed on the cross looking down on the Sea of Galilee. There was a plaster copy of Nefertiti on his desk, along with a statue of a horse and a heavy black typewriter. The bookshelves held a couple hundred books, mostly theology and rows of biblical commentaries. He did not read much fiction; indeed his favorite novel, which was a source of some embarrassment to me, was *All Things Bright and Beautiful*. His office, across the driveway from our house, was a sanctuary. He was a gentle man, almost always in a cheerful mood, and had endless patience for his three children. His black robe hung on a hanger on the back of his office door. I could usually smell the black printing fluid from the ditto machine, used to roll off the weekly church bulletins. On Saturday nights we were often there, cranking out the bulletins and folding them for the Sunday service.

He was always impeccably dressed in a dark suit with a clerical collar or a tie. As I grew older he despaired of my slovenliness. He took me when I came home from college—he then had a church in Syracuse—to meet his Italian tailor, a man who fitted his Brooks Brothers suits. The visit did not cure my indifference to fashion. He painted landscapes and still life. He organized events for the elderly ladies in the church, and once again, to my great embarrassment, created a flower arrangement with them that won the town flower-arranging competition. He was a man who hated conflict. But he accepted it for the rest of his life, when no doubt his inclination was to turn away.

The rumblings of the civil rights movement were slow to reach our town. There were no people of color, although the balcony in the church had been built for slaves. Those African-Americans had been erased from our collective memory, a cultural and historical genocide that I later saw in the Middle East and the

Balkans. This erasure is part of many New England towns. There was no African-American cemetery. There were no pictures of African-Americans on display in the Old Stone Fort, which served as our local museum. When we read the history of our valley, of the struggles by the German and Dutch settlers against the Mohawk Indians, we heard only about self-reliance, resilience and courage. The African-American men and women, who were also here, were never mentioned. We censored and erased huge chunks of our past to create myth in the guise of history.

In the early 1960s Dr. Martin Luther King was one of the most hated men in America. His message of equality was viewed as subversive, a message many in the town felt would undermine our way of life. My father and mother's early embrace of the movement, and of Dr. King in particular, rankled some in the church. It came up when I went to get my hair cut down the street, with the old men sitting around quizzing me. It came up at school, where kids teased me about it. It came up at home, where my father told me that doing what was right was not comfortable. Moral choice, he said, always entailed risk. If there was no risk it was probably not moral.

Advocating civil rights, even in our town, was one thing. Opposing the Vietnam War was worse. I do not remember rousing sermons against the war; this was not my father's style. But his opposition to the war was known. The cutting remarks I heard about him burned inside of me, fostering an anger that would see the son, unlike the father, spend his life searching out conflict and relishing the ability to strike back. I soon understood that you could not expect to be rewarded for moral choice. Such choice, in fact, usually generated anger and hatred.

My father's youngest brother was gay. He lived with his partner in Greenwich Village and worked in the shoe department of Lord & Taylor. We never discussed his sexuality. I was a teenager before it dawned on me that my uncle and his partner were lovers. It was not something I wanted to think much about, but it would mark the last phase of my life with my father.

Colgate University is an hour from Syracuse, where my father had his last church. He visited frequently to take me to lunch or watch me act in school plays. He soon noticed there was no gay and lesbian student group on campus and so he brought gay speakers to my college. The meetings, which I attended, saw me sitting with my father among small groups of students and the invited speakers. I counted the minutes until the sessions ended. But it meant a lot to the gay students who lived an underground, clandestine existence.

My father, over lunch, told me that since student groups could not be founded anonymously, and since none of the gay or lesbian students wanted to go public, I would have to found the campus gay and lesbian organization. I dutifully formed the group that met each week under my name, although I never attended. The student who checked us in for meals at the dining hall would mark my card and hand it back saying "faggot."

My uncle was living with his partner running an antiques shop in Maine when he died. My father slipped a ring off his brother's hand, a coiled serpent, which he had sent him from Iran during the war. All I remember him saying after the funeral was "poor thing." He knew, as well as anyone who did not directly suffer discrimination, what it meant to be an outsider, a dissident, a poor, uneducated white man or woman, a minority, a gay or lesbian. He knew the awful cost of being different, the intolerance and hatred it bred, the way it leads us to deny the humanity of others, perhaps because of our own hidden differences, our fear that we too will be thrust aside by the crowd.

But what struck me about him most, as I grew older, is that he did not have to embrace difference. Charming, good looking, endowed with an infectious sense of humor, it would have been easier to go along. He could have simply been "nice." He could have avoided the confrontations that tore him apart. But he understood the message of the gospel, although I suspect his actions were less intellectual than instinctual. I asked him once when I was a teenager what he said to bereaved families when he went to the farmhouses after the funerals of loved ones. Surely, I thought, even my father with his close proximity to disease and death and grief would have some wisdom to impart.

"Mostly," he answered, "I make the coffee."

I had some disdain for his answer then, but I honor it now. There is little to do in the face of death but make the coffee. We have no words to blunt its awfulness. It was his presence, more than anything he could say, which mattered.

At the end of William Shakespeare's *Love's Labor's Lost,* the young men who have wooed the princesses of France are confronted in their courtship with the sudden death of the French king. When the King of Navarre attempts to continue the courtship, the princess of France, reeling after the news of the death of her father, says: "I understand you not, my griefs are double."[1] We can remember the departed with words, but the presence of death defies articulation. Berowne, whose wit and verbal dexterity allow him to justify perjury and the breaking of vows of chastity and obedience, is told by Rosaline, the woman he loves, that he must work for a year in a charnel house before asking again for his lady's hand.

> *Rosaline.* You shall this twelvemonth term from day to day
> Visit the speechless sick, and still converse
> With groaning wretches; and your task shall be,
> With all the fierce endeavor of your wit,
> To enforce the pained impotent to smile.
> *Berowne.* To move wild laughter in the throat of death?
> It cannot be, it is impossible . . . [2]

The play ends with the cryptic sentence: "The words of Mercury are harsh after the songs of Apollo."[3] A potent reminder that even Apollo, the god of poetry, is rendered mute by nonbeing.

On October 26, 1995, I was watching *Tosca* at the Belgrade

Opera. I spent the the night after the performance drinking with most of the cast in a restaurant called La Scala. It had a small band. The cast sang arias and Russian and Serbian folk songs, accompanied by the house band, until early in the morning. Serbian officers, the double eagles and signs of rank on their uniforms, men who may well have been in charge of the artillery and snipers who rained death upon us in Sarajevo a few weeks earlier, wept and joined the chorus. One of the officers, seeing that I was a guest, took his silver double-headed eagle off his hat and gave it to me as a gift. I did not know it, but at that moment my father was dying.

Tosca and the war in Bosnia were intertwined. During the nighttime explosions in Sarajevo I sat alone in my room in the Holiday Inn, its front sheered off by artillery fire. I shuddered with the explosions. I went to the sprawling black market, where desperate city residents were selling anything to survive, to buy a stereo. I found an old system and went to hunt for something to play. There was little music to be found in a city that lacked running water and was beset by food shortages, but I managed to buy the second of two discs from Puccini's *Tosca*. When the night shelling began I cranked up the stereo to drown out the heavy guns. I listened, night after night, to Acts II and III, where Cavaradossi, Tosca's lover, is tortured by Scarpia's police. Tosca, forced to listen to her lover's cries of agony, is told that she must sleep with Scarpia or see her lover killed. Overcome by grief she falls onto the settee under Scarpia's cold gaze and sings:

> *I have lived for art, I have lived for love,*
> *and never harmed a living soul!*
> *In secret I have given aid*
> *to as many unfortunates as I have known.*
> *Always a true believer,*
> *I have offered up my prayers*
> *at the holy shrines;*

always a true believer,
I have laid flowers on the altar.
In my hour of tribulation
why, O Lord, why
hast Thou repaid me thus?[4]

Then she stabs and kills Scarpia, who sings "Help! . . . I'm dying! . . . Help! . . . I'm dying! . . ."[5] These words were being echoed when I listened to them in the bleak, bombed-out remains of Sarajevo, where death was a constant companion. I thought always of the mortally wounded, lying in the darkness under rubble. Tosca flees the scene of the murder to witness her lover's execution. She leaps, herself pursued, from the ramparts to her death.

When I returned to the hotel there was a message to call home. My father had died from a heart attack. I preached, as he had done for his own family, at his funeral. There was no coffin. He was clear about not having his body, even in a closed coffin, on display. And then we buried him on a hilltop in Maine next to my small house that looks out over the White Mountains in New Hampshire. He was gone.

What does it mean to honor a father? It is not to become him, not to search for him, which those who lost fathers or mothers young in life, or never knew them, often set out to do. In the wars I covered, from El Salvador to the Balkans, there would periodically appear a young man or woman whose father had been killed working as a correspondent or photographer. These men and women were especially unfit for the hard, cynical world of war, with its black humor and insensitivity, which enveloped and deformed us. We were not what they were looking to find. They retreated from what they saw, although what they saw was often an accurate reflection of what they had lost. These encounters broke my heart. I saw my son or daughter looking for me, looking for the gentle smile of a father in the faces of men and women numbed and hardened by too much violent death.

All parents, for better or worse, shape our lives. They condition our responses years after they are gone. Children who were loved, or not loved, who yearned for approval that was never sufficient, who fled the harsh oppression of the home, who rejected all their parents had pressed down on them until they became, as if in a cruel reversal, simply what their parents were not, live out these yearnings as adults. Or maybe they can never leave the embrace of home at all, living years later under the protective and suffocating love of the parent. But the imprint is unavoidable. It marks us into old age.

We all honor our parents, even parents we reject, even parents whose cruelty did not make them fit to be called parents. For to honor our parents is to honor our essence, the roots from which we sprung, and even the best parents have an oppressive power that must be broken. We must free ourselves from our parents to become fully formed individuals, in the process taking with us that which they gave us, or did not give us, and trying to fashion a distinct and separate life. It is a life that must, in the end, replace the parent. And as our children grow we look into the face of our own decline, our eventual death.

None of the commandments were written for children. They were written for adults. The commandment to honor your parents is a commandment to honor yourself, honor the life force that created you, the good and the bad mingled within us, but not to honor abuse. Those who were abused, who wince at the name of father or mother, cannot be asked to honor the memory of the abuse or the abuser. But at the same time, however painful, we have to see in parents, even bad parents, reflections of ourselves, if only to guard against and keep at bay the demons within us. We cannot wish our parents away. They will always be a major, overpowering force in our life. We cannot undo abuse, but we can find a way to honor life, even their lives, by turning that abuse into compassion not only for ourselves, which is necessary for healing, but more important for all who suffer. Those who use personal pain to mitigate the pain of others, who take the experience of sorrow and the suffering and use it to lead a life of compassion, honor their parents, even as they rise above them. They honor life, which is what their parents gave them. They honor what is holy and good. They take out of tragedy a regenerative power. They fulfill the commandment. We all carry, imprinted on our faces, like the mark of Cain, our origins, our link with the past, wanted or unwanted. We cannot wash it away. It is rather a matter of what we do with it, how we honor it, how we redeem the experience to protect and create life.

"One day it will be realized that men are distinguishable as much by the forms their memories take as by their characters,"[6] wrote André Malraux.

Memories define us. Charon the grim ferryman of Greek myth, who took the souls of the dead from the banks of the Lethe to the underworld, forced his passengers to drink from the river. The waters of the Lethe erased memory. It obliterated all that makes us distinct, all that makes it possible to love, to understand, to react, to form our lives and our relationships. Without memory we as distinct individuals cease to exist. And memory, the good and the bad, are part of our long continuum. We are the product of a chain of human folly and greed, of scoundrels and saints, of love and passion, of hurts and joys. Our memories define us, define us even as we turn on some memories and honor others.

My father gave me freedom. He taught me that to make a moral choice means taking a risk, even as it means losing status within the institutions you work for, or losing status within your community. It can mean suffering the censure of people you care about. But when we care too much about our image and our status, when we need the label of the institutions we work for, including the church, to define our worth and identity, when we allow these things to become the ultimate source of meaning in our lives, we worship idols. We allow idols to determine what we say and how we act, how we make moral choices, how we live. Fearing the wrath of the idol we remain silent in the face of injustice or perhaps carry out injustice. We give up our freedom.

My father never spoke to me about my decision not to be ordained. It must have been hard. I had completed divinity school. All that stood between me and ordination were the exams, which would have been easily passed. I turned my back on the church, on the institution that had defined his life. When I graduated from seminary to leave for El Salvador to cover the war he told me I was "ordained to write."

Our lives circle back, unconsciously, sometimes consciously to our origin. I found myself in pulpits, of sorts, during the war in Iraq. I had to decide how to speak, what I was willing to risk, how far I was willing to go, what language I would employ. I remembered my father.

On a May afternoon in 2003 in Rockford, Illinois, I stood before about 1,000 guests to deliver the commencement address at Rockford College. I knew nothing about the school, other than that its most famous and celebrated alumnus was Jane Addams, the feminist, socialist and pacifist founder of Hull House in Chicago who was excoriated for denouncing World War I. The students read her writings. But many in the crowd, and the administration, while they may have been able to honor her memory, had no stomach for honoring her ideals.

The address, built around my book, *War Is a Force That Gives Us Meaning,* was a critique of the war in Iraq, one that was delivered with the hammer blows of a man who had been trained as a preacher. The mood of the crowd, indeed of much of the country, was not ready for a denunciation of the Iraqi war. President Bush had, not long before, landed on an aircraft carrier and stood in front of a banner that read "Mission Accomplished." The country was imbibing the heady brew of victory, seeing in the swift defeat of the Iraqis an empowering military and moral superiority that rendered us great and good. Arrogance and triumphalism poisoned our discourse.

I walked to the podium at the end of the line of faculty. I wore a borrowed black robe and a borrowed academic hood. It was windy. We climbed the steps and took our seats. The graduating class sat in folding chairs in the front. The audience was behind them. There were black speaker boxes mounted on poles to broadcast the ceremony.

When it was time for my address I walked to the podium. My left hand held down the papers so they would not be scattered by the breeze. I began:

I want to speak to you today about war and empire.

The killing, or at least the worst of it, is over in Iraq. Although blood will continue to spill—theirs and ours—be prepared for this. For we are embarking on an occupation that, if history is any guide, will be as damaging to our souls as it will be to our prestige, power and security. But this will come later as our empire expands. And in all this we become pariahs, tyrants to others weaker than ourselves. Isolation always impairs judgment, and we are very isolated now.

We have forfeited the goodwill, the empathy the world felt for us after 9/11. We have folded in on ourselves, we have severely weakened the delicate international coalitions and alliances that are vital in maintaining and promoting peace. And we are part now of a dubious troika in the war against terror with Vladimir Putin and Ariel Sharon, two leaders who do not shrink in Palestine or Chechnya from carrying out gratuitous and senseless acts of violence. We have become the company we keep.

The censure, and perhaps the rage, of much of the world—certainly one-fifth of the world's population which is Muslim, most of whom I will remind you are not Arab—is upon us. Look today at the fourteen people killed last night in several explosions in Casablanca. And this rage, in a world where almost fifty percent of the planet struggles on less than two dollars a day, will see us targeted. Terrorism will become a way of life. [Someone in the crowd shouts, "No!"] *And when we are attacked, we will, like our allies Putin and Sharon, lash out with greater fury.*

The circle of violence is a death spiral; no one escapes. We are spinning at a speed that we may not be able to halt. As we revel in our military prowess—the sophistication of our military hardware and technology, for this is what most of the press coverage consisted of in Iraq—we lose sight of the fact that just because we have the capacity to wage war it does not give us the right to wage war. This capacity has doomed empires in the past.

"Modern western civilization may perish," the theologian Reinhold Niebuhr warned, *"because it falsely worshipped technology as a final good."*

The real injustices—the Israeli occupation of Palestinian land, the brutal and corrupt dictatorships we fund in the Middle East—will mean that we will not rid the extremists who hate us with bombs. Indeed, we will swell their ranks. [Whistles.] *Once you master people by force you depend on force for control. In your isolation you begin to make mistakes.* ["Where were you on September eleven?"]

Fear engenders cruelty; cruelty . . . fear, insanity, and then paralysis. [Hoots. "Who wants to listen to this jerk?"] *In the center of Dante's circle the damned remained motionless.* [Horns.] *We have blundered into a nation we know little about and are caught between bitter rivalries and competing ethnic groups and leaders we do not understand. We are trying to transplant a modern system of politics invented in Europe characterized, among other things, by the division of earth into independent secular states based on national citizenship in a land where the belief in a secular civil government is an alien creed. Iraq was a cesspool for the British when they occupied it in 1917. It will be a cesspool for us, as well.* ["God bless America," a woman yells.] *The curfews, the armed clashes with angry crowds that leave scores of Iraqi dead, the military governor, the Christian Evangelical groups who are being allowed to follow on the heels of our occupying troops to try and teach Muslims about Jesus, the occupation of the oilfields . . .*

[At this point someone unplugs the microphone. When it is fixed, Rockford College President Paul C. Pribbenow addresses the audience: "My friends, one of the wonders of a liberal arts college is its ability and its deeply held commitment to academic freedom and the decision to listen to each other's opinions. If you wish to protest the speaker's remarks, I ask that you do it in silence, as some of you are doing in the back. That is perfectly appropriate, but he has the right to offer his opinion here, and we would like him to continue his remarks." People blow horns and boo and some applaud.]

The occupation of the oilfields. [More boos. A woman says, "We're not going to listen. We've listened enough. You've already ruined our graduation. Don't ruin it any more, sir."] *The notion that the Kurds and the Shiites will listen to the demands of a centralized government in Baghdad—the same Kurds and Shiites who died by the tens of thousands in defiance of Saddam Hussein, a man who happily butchered all of those who challenged him, and this ethnic rivalry has not gone away. The looting of Baghdad, or let me say the looting of Baghdad with the exception of the oil ministry and the interior ministry—the only two ministries we bothered protecting—is self-immolation.* [More boos.]

    As someone who knows Iraq, speaks Arabic, and spent seven years in the Middle East, if the Iraqis believe rightly or wrongly that we come only for oil and occupation, they will begin a long, bloody war of attrition. It is how they drove the British out. And remember that, when the Israelis invaded southern Lebanon in 1982, they were greeted by the dispossessed Shiites as liberators, but within a few months, when the Shiites saw that the Israelis had come not as liberators but as occupiers, they began to kill them. It was Israel who created Hezbollah, and it was Hezbollah that pushed Israel out of southern Lebanon.

As William Butler Yeats wrote in "Meditations in Time of Civil War," "We had fed the heart on fantasies / The heart's grown brutal from the fare." [Horns. "I never would have come if I knew I had to listen to this," a woman yells.]

This is a war of liberation in Iraq, but it is a war now of liberation by Iraqis from American occupation. And if you watch closely what is happening in Iraq, if you can see it through the abysmal coverage, you can see it in the lashing out of the terrorist death squads, the murder of Shiite leaders in mosques, and the assassination of our young soldiers in the streets. It is one that will soon be joined by Islamic radicals and we are far less secure today than we were before we bumbled into Iraq. ["USA, USA," some in the crowd chant.]

We will pay for this, but what saddens me most is that those who will, by and large, pay the highest price are poor kids from Mississippi or Alabama or Texas who could not get a decent job or health insurance and joined the army because it was all we offered them. For war in the end is always about betrayal, betrayal of the young by the old, of soldiers by politicians, and of idealists by cynics.

Read Antigone, when the king imposes his will without listening to those he rules, or Thucydides' history. [Heckling.] *Read how Athens' expanding empire saw it become a tyrant abroad and then a tyrant at home, how the tyranny the Athenian leadership imposed on others it finally imposed on itself.*

This, Thucydides wrote, is what doomed Athenian democracy; Athens destroyed itself. For the instrument of empire is war, and war is a poison, a poison which at times we must ingest just as a cancer patient must ingest a poison to survive. But if we do not understand the poison of war—if we do not understand how deadly that poison is—it can kill us just as surely as the disease. ["It's enough, it's enough, it's enough," a woman says.]

We have lost touch with the essence of war. Following our defeat in Vietnam we became a better nation. We were humbled, even humiliated. We asked questions about ourselves we had not asked before.

We were forced to see ourselves as others saw us, and the sight was not always a pretty one. We were forced to confront our own capacity for atrocity—for evil—and in this we understood not only war but more about ourselves. But that humility is gone.

War, we have come to believe, is a spectator sport. The military and the press—remember in wartime the press is always part of the problem—have turned war into a vast video arcade game. Its very essence—death—is hidden from public view.

There was no more candor in the Persian Gulf War or the war in Afghanistan or the war in Iraq than there was in Vietnam. [Horns.] *But in the age of live feeds and satellite television, the state and the military have perfected the appearance of candor.* [Heckling.]

Because we no longer understand war, we no longer understand that it can all go horribly wrong. We no longer understand that war begins by calling for the annihilation of others but ends, if we do not know when to make or maintain peace, with self-annihilation. We flirt, given the potency of modern weapons, with our own destruction. ["That's not true!"]

The seduction of war is insidious because so much of what we are told about it is true: it does create a feeling of comradeship, which obliterates our alienation and makes us, for perhaps the only time of our life, feel we belong.

War allows us to rise above our small stations in life. We find nobility in a cause and feelings of selflessness and even bliss. And at a time of soaring deficits and financial scandals and the very deterioration of our domestic fabric, war is a fine diversion. War, for those who enter into combat, has a dark beauty, filled with the monstrous and the grotesque. The Bible calls it the lust of the eye and warns believers against it. War gives us a distorted sense of self; it gives us meaning. [Shouts of "Go home!" Then a man in the audience climbs to the stage and says, "Can I say a few words here?" I respond, "When I finish— yeah, when I finish."]

Once in war, the conflict obliterates the past and the future. All is one heady intoxicating present. You feel every heartbeat in war, colors are brighter, your mind races ahead of itself.

[Boos, and the microphone is unplugged momentarily again. "Should I keep going?" I ask President Pribbenow, who responds, "It's up to you." I ask, "Do you want me to stop?" Pribbenow says, "How close are you? Why don't you bring it to a close?" More shouts of "Go home!" One person says, "It's not your graduation." Some, now weeping, begin to sing "God Bless America."]

We feel in wartime comradeship. [Many loud boos.] *We confuse this with friendship, with love. There are those who will insist that the comradeship of war is love. The exotic glow that makes us in war feel as one people, one entity, is real, but this is part of war's intoxication.* [More boos.]

Think back on the days after the attacks on nine-eleven. Suddenly we no longer felt alone; we connected with strangers, even with people we did not like. We felt we belonged, that we were somehow wrapped in the embrace of the nation, the community. In short, we no longer felt alienated. ["Go home!"]

As this feeling dissipated in the weeks after the attack, there was a kind of nostalgia for its warm glow. And wartime always brings with it this comradeship, which is the opposite of friendship. Friends, as J. Glenn Gray points out, are predetermined; friendship takes place between men and women who possess an intellectual and emotional affinity for each other. But comradeship—that ecstatic bliss that comes with belonging to the crowd in wartime—is within our reach. We can all have comrades.

The danger of the external threat that comes when we have an enemy does not create friendship; it creates comradeship. And those in wartime are deceived about what they are undergoing. And this is why once the threat is over, once war ends, comrades again become strangers to us. This is why, after war, we fall into despair. ["Atheist stranger!"]

In friendship there is a deepening of our sense of self. We become, through the friend, more aware of who we are and what we are about; we find ourselves in the eyes of the friend. Friends probe and question and

*challenge each other to make each of us more complete. In comradeship,
the kind that comes to us in patriotic fervor, there is a suppression of self-
awareness, self-knowledge and self-possession.* [Heckling.] *Comrades
lose their identities in wartime for the collective rush of a common
cause—a common purpose. In comradeship there are no demands on the
self. This is part of its appeal and one of the reasons we miss it and seek to
recreate it.* ["Go home! Go home!"] *Comradeship allows us to escape
the demands on the self that is part of friendship.*

*In wartime when we feel threatened, we no longer face death alone but
as a group, and this makes death easier to bear. We ennoble self-sacrifice
for the other, for the comrade.* [Boos.] *In short we begin to worship
death. And this is what the god of war demands of us.*

*Think finally of what it means to die for a friend. It is deliberate and
painful; there is no ecstasy. For friends, dying is hard and bitter. The dia-
logue they have and cherish will perhaps never be recreated. Friends do
not, the way comrades do, love death and sacrifice. To friends, the prospect
of death is frightening. And this is why friendship—or, let me say love—is
the most potent enemy of war. Thank you.*

[There are boos, whistles, horn blasts and a smattering of
applause. "This is the most destructive thing you've ever
done to this college, Dr. Pribbenow," says a woman. "You
should never have allowed him to speak."][7]

I sat down in the chair behind the podium. I opened a small plastic bottle of water. The awarding of the diplomas began. A heavy-
set man who identified himself as the head of campus security
asked me to climb off the stage and follow him. I was put in a car
and driven to my hotel. I packed my bags, was handed the coat I
had left in the president's office and put on a bus to Chicago.

The event spawned a feeding frenzy among conservative com-
mentators from Rush Limbaugh to his well-groomed counter-
parts on Fox News. *The Wall Street Journal* ran an editorial

denouncing the talk. The local paper, *The Rockford Register Star,* reported the event with the headline SPEAKER DISRUPTS RC GRADUATION.

I gave few interviews. I refused the invitations to go on television talk shows. I did not want to toss little bits of red meat into the public arena to keep the story alive.

The New York Times, my employer, sent me a letter of reprimand, saying I had made "public remarks that could undermine public trust in the paper's impartiality." I was called into the office. It was an unpleasant moment. We all fear losing our job. We all fear insecurity. We dislike angering those above us. I am no different. But I knew what I was called to do. I had seen the cost.

To be silent would be to betray my father, to turn my back on what he stood for, to deny his life, to dishonor his memory, to dishonor my own memory. The physical resurrection of Jesus from the dead is not the only story of resurrection in the Gospels. A few weeks after the crucifixion in Acts, two disciples, who had fled Jesus on the night of the arrest, were hauled before the authorities for preaching. This time they refused to betray Jesus. This refusal was a physical manifestation of the resurrection, of new life.

I am not sure my father, as a distinct individual, exists in death, although I dream of him frequently. I am not sure he knows what has happened to his son. I doubt he can hear my voice, but then he does not need to. It is his own. I am my father's son. This is my inheritance. I will not squander it.

MURDER

You shall not kill.

Bishop George Packard has a burden. He carries it with him. There are times in his sleep when it overpowers him and wakes him, leaving him to wrestle through the night with shadows. There are days when stress mounts, the memories suddenly bursting around him in unpleasant succession. And in the ticking of the clock, the race toward oblivion that is the fate of all human beings, he seeks atonement in everything he does as a husband, a father and an Episcopal priest.

He grew up on Long Island in a middle-class, churchgoing home. He went to Hobart College in upstate New York, graduated, got married, went to law school for a year and then heard "the hoof beats of my draft board." He enlisted and was sent, after basic training, to become an officer at Fort Benning.

The war was not entirely unwelcome. He had never been much of a student, nor a star athlete, although adequate. He realized during his first year at law school that "the Lord probably had other things in mind for me." He knew a little of uniforms and duty, having been a Boy Scout. It seemed good preparation. He had been a camp counselor. He saw war as an adventure.

I drove to his suburban house north of New York. We sat in a sunken living room with polished wooden floors and mission-style furniture. Christmas was a few days away. There was an Advent candle waiting to be lit with his daughter, in the wreath on the table. He wore the purple bib of a bishop and a clerical collar.

"I was not reflective about it," he said. "I liked the outdoors, being part of a troop, being a body in a platoon. I liked that feeling of corporate identity. I figured I knew the lifestyle."

He led his first ambush in 1969, 20 days after he arrived in Vietnam. As he stood over the bodies he viewed them with a disquieting lack of emotion.

"'In the war movies you see soldiers vomit after they kill for the first time," he said. "I looked at those I had killed and knew it should have been overwhelming, but I felt only that I had accomplished my task. The army trains you well to make you do extraordinary things under fire. There is no bravery on a battlefield."

He soon learned that the cries of the wounded North Vietnamese or Vietcong soldiers had to be silenced swiftly and ruthlessly so his unit could avoid detection. Compassion was a luxury he could not afford.

"I would throw area grenades at the wounded until they were dead," he said. "I remember in one firefight killing a man who crawled toward me with his legs blown off. It was not pretty."

His first thought, once the shooting stopped—a thought he now finds strange—was how to tell others about the clash. He began, in the minutes after a firefight, to give a coherency to the violence that took place around him, to make the chaos into a story, make it fit the movie running in his head.

In the half-light of the mornings, he said, he and his men went through pockets of the bodies. He often found photographs, reminders that those he had killed had mothers, fathers, wives, children and lovers. The unit once discovered the picture of a young blond woman on a body, most likely taken from an American the North Vietnamese soldier had killed in an earlier firefight.

He would collect the pictures he found on the bodies after each firefight and make a little pile on the ground.

"I burned the pictures I found, although no one in my platoon saw me do this, because I felt that I had in my possession tokens of the lives of those I had killed," he said. "I held in my hands something precious, something ultimate that I had taken away from another human being. I have often thought about trying to find the girlfriends or the parents of those I killed and write to say I was sorry."

David Rogers was a conscientious objector who worked as the platoon's medic. He helped search the dead bodies, turning over documents to intelligence officers, keeping gear such as the coveted "gook ponchos" for the rain. The medic and the lieutenant worked in tandem, sorting out the new recruits to see who would be good killers and who would not.

"We told all the new recruits coming into the unit that the medic had to check their feet," said Packard. "It was a ruse. Rogers would speak to them as he looked at their feet and then give me a signal to let me know if they were any good or I should get rid of them."

War unleashed widespread industrial slaughter. It swept through the jungles of Southeast Asia. Villages were put to flame, water buffaloes were shot for sport, human beings were machine-gunned from the air and grenades were tossed down tunnels where women and children, rather than guerrilla fighters, huddled in fear. The soldiers had at their fingertips the heady ability to call in air strikes and firepower that turned farming villages with thatch-roofed huts into fiery infernos. War brought to Packard power to give or deprive human life. This power made him sick and demented. The world was turned upside down. He and his soldiers, with the power to spare or deprive life, felt like gods.

The perversion of the war in Vietnam spawned sexual abuse

and prostitution, black markets and dope, and a cacaphony of lies told to wage war. Human beings became objects. Life was reduced to a vortex of pain or ecstasy. Law was of no consequence. In a firefight, afraid and pumped up with adrenaline and excitement, they became agents of death.

"Where was God in Vietnam?" he asked himself.

It is the question all who have been to war face, for war is a godless endeavor. When love, compassion and human kindness are replaced by the vast, grotesque panorama of violence and destruction of war, God is banished. Human beings, who have the freedom to choose good and evil, can not find within them the power of the divine when they embrace a world of sin. At that moment they shut out the divine. And war is a state of almost unadulterated sin.

"Killing is always dirty," said the former medic Rogers, who spoke with me reluctantly. "You never get over it. There was an endless counting of the dead. If you killed you knew you would be killed. It evened out. You would walk away from blood on the grass and you understood that you could be killed next time. There was no perfect choice; just because I was a medic does not mean I was not part of the killing."

Packard spent a year as an army lieutenant leading platoons. He and his men killed in each encounter anywhere from 12 to 15 North Vietnamese, Vietcong and perhaps Chinese mercenaries. They did it clinically and efficiently. He said he stopped counting how many young men and boys he killed. "But with about thirty ambushes and firefights you can do the math," he said.

He was good at what he did. It horrifies him now, but there was a part of him that enjoyed it. There was a part of him that liked to kill, that sought out the high of combat like a junkie heading down to the park to find another fix. War was at once revolting and seductive.

"I violated the commandment, 'Thou Shalt Not Kill.' Nothing will be gained by intellectualizing this. I killed other people. I took lives. It was exactly that. I became in Vietnam a professional killer. I was proud of what I could do. There are days when I meet with people, trying to do what is good for the church, for others, and think I am probably the only person here who has killed another human being."

He received the Silver Star and two Bronze Stars for valor. He spent his last months in the army teaching ambush tactics to army rangers. But he returned home disillusioned, "hating the war." He entered the seminary in 1971, not sure that he wanted to be a priest, but "to study the ethical and moral issues that confronted me in Vietnam." There was little time for questioning in Vietnam. He began to look back on what he had done. He felt guilty.

Bishop Packard discovered in the war the capacity we all have for evil. He discovered the darkness that allows us, when the restraints are cut, to commit acts of brutality against the weak and the defenseless, including children. He discovered the ghoulish delight soldiers can take in killing. He discovered that all is not right with the world, as he had been taught, that honoring nation and family and a God that leads us to victory and righteousness and success, does not mean we will be saved or indeed victorious or even successful. He discovered the lie he had been told, the idolatry of our civic religion, one that grafts the will to power onto the will of God. And in this knowledge he made a painful self-discovery, not only about himself but about the human race. His naive belief in the goodness of the nation and the individual, one that gave him, as it gives all of us, comfort and moral certainty, was obliterated in Vietnam. He peered into the American soul and what he saw looking back horrified him. But out of that pain and alienation came knowledge, a need to reclaim life. The darkness he confronted became his cross. He carries it every day.

He learned that few wanted to hear what he had endured, what he had learned. The antiwar activists attacked him for going to Vietnam, but in their self-righteousness did not understand that the darkness he encountered was the darkness that dwells in all of us. He challenged the myth of a great and moral nation, a nation ordained by God to carry out a civilizing mission through violence. He angered believers, those who sought their meaning and identity in the myth of war as noble and glorious. He and other Vietnam veterans found they were unwanted in local VFW halls. He was lonely, able only to relate to those who had been in Vietnam. But he had returned home like a biblical prophet, to speak a painful truth about us, a truth few wanted to hear. The cost of this knowledge was catastrophic.

> *After such knowledge, what forgiveness? Think now*
> *History has many cunning passages, contrived corridors*
> *And issues, deceives with whispering ambitions,*
> *Guides us by vanities. . . .*
> *Think*
> *Neither fear nor courage saves us. Unnatural vices*
> *Are fathered by our heroism. Virtues*
> *Are forced upon us by our impudent crimes.*
> *These tears are shaken from the wrath-bearing tree.*[1]

When he cannot sleep, which is often, the bishop thinks about the widows and children without fathers, or the wives and children they should have had. He thinks about the agony of final moments when soldiers bled to death in front of him. He sees faces before him of the long dead. He wants to reach out to them, but they recede in front of him, insubstantial spirits. He wonders if they can forgive him. He prays for this. He wonders if he can forgive himself.

We make our heroes out of clay. We laud their gallant deeds and give them uniforms with colored ribbons on their chests for the acts of violence they committed or endured. They are our repositories of glory, of power, of self-righteousness, of patriotism and self-worship, all that we want to believe about ourselves. They are our plaster saints of war, the icons we cheer to defend us and empower us. They are products of our civic religion, our worship of power and force, our blind belief in our right as a chosen nation to wield this force against the weak. This is our nation's idolatry of itself. This idolatry has corrupted our religious institutions, as in many nations. It has made it hard for us to separate the will of God from the will of the state. The state becomes God's agent. Religion becomes a tool for those in power.

Those who returned from Vietnam disrupted our love affair with ourselves, with our power and self-righteousness. We cast them out like lepers. We condemned returning veterans for their spiritual and physical mutilations. We listened only when they spoke from the script we handed them. If they told us of terrible wounds visible and invisible, of the lies used to justify killing, it was hard to bear. Not our boys, many said, not them, bred in our homes, endowed with goodness and decency. For if it is easy for them to murder, what about us? And so it is simpler not to see. We stopped listening to the angry words that poured from their lips, wishing only that they would calm down, be reasonable, get some help, and go away. We, who did not want to look, branded our prophets as madmen. We cast them into the desert. And we left many alone and enraged.

Wars come wrapped in patriotic slogans, calls for self-sacrifice and glory. They come wrapped in the claims of divine providence. It is what a nation asks of its young. It is what is right and just. War is always waged, we were told, to make the nation and the world a better place, to cleanse evil. War is touted as the ultimate test of manhood, where young men can find out what they are made of. War gives us comrades and power. It gives us a chance to play a small bit in the great drama of history. It promises to give us an identity as a warrior, a patriot, as long as we go along with the myth, the one the war-makers use to wage war.

But up close war is a soulless void. War quickly descends to raw barbarity, perversion, pain and an unchecked orgy of death. It is a state where human decency and tenderness are crushed, where those who make war work overtime to destroy love, where all human beings become objects to use or kill. The noise, the stench, the fear, the eviscerated bodies and bloated corpses, the crying wounded spin us into another universe. In this moral void, blessed by institutions at home, the hypocrisy of our social conventions are laid bare. We call for strict adherence to some commandments and laud the purposeful violation of others. Hypocrisy rules. War, for all its horror, has the power to strip away the trivial and the banal, the empty chatter and foolish obsessions. It lets us see.

The Reverend William P. Mahedy, a Catholic chaplain in Vietnam, tells of a soldier, a former altar boy, in his book *Out of the Night: The Spiritual Journey of Vietnam Vets,* who says to him: "Hey, Chaplain, . . . how come it's a sin to hop into bed with a *mama-san* but it's okay to blow away gooks out in the bush?"[2]

"Consider the question that he and I were forced to confront on that day in a jungle clearing," Mahedy writes. "How is it that a Christian can, with a clear conscience, spend a year in a war zone killing people and yet place his soul in jeopardy by spending a few minutes with a prostitute? If the New Testament prohibitions of sexual misconduct are to be stringently interpreted, why, then, are Jesus' injunctions against violence not binding in the same way? In other words, what does the commandment 'Thou shalt not kill' really mean?"[3]

Of all the commandments that are broken, the Torah says, only those who murder can not be certain of forgiveness. For forgiveness, the Torah says, can only be granted by the murdered victim. Murder leaves a stain. It marks you. The Hebrew word "to kill" or "rsh" appears in the Hebrew Bible 46 times and the commandment is probably better translated as "do not murder," although this remains debated by biblical scholars. There is a difference between killing someone who is trying to kill you and killing someone who does not have the power to harm you. The first is killing. The second is murder. But murder, in insurgencies like Vietnam and Iraq, often becomes more common than killing.

Killing and murder are each sinful. Those who kill, even in self-defense, must cope with terrible trauma and guilt. Murder, however, can corrode and ruin the lives of those we send into war. The failure of religious institutions, whose texts are unequivocal about murder, to address in times of war the sinful state of war has left them unable to speak to the reality of war. These institutions have little or nothing to say in wartime because the god they worship is often a false god, one that promises victory to those who obey the law and believe in the manifest destiny of the nation. The god of war takes over the pulpits and the airwaves. Religious leaders line up to bless the enterprise of war.

We all have the capacity to commit evil. It takes little to unleash it. For those of us who have been to war this is the knowledge that is hardest to digest, the knowledge that the line between the victims and the victimizers is razor thin, that human beings find a perverse delight in destruction and death and few can resist the pull.

Wars may have to be fought to ensure survival, but they are always tragic, always sinful. They always bring to the surface the worst elements of a society, those who have a penchant for violence and a lust for absolute power. It was the criminal class that first organized the defense of Sarajevo. And when these criminals were not manning roadblocks to hold off the besieging Bosnian Serb army, they were looting, raping and killing the Serb residents in the city. War exposes "original sin," or the "sin of the world." And those who speak of war as an instrument of power, those who wage war but do not know its reality, those powerful politicians and statesmen, the Henry Kissingers, Robert McNamaras, Donald Rumsfelds, those who treat war as part of the great game of nations, are amoral. When the wars are over they have nothing to say to us in their thick memoirs about war, for they know nothing of war.

"In theological terms, war is sin," writes Mahedy. "This has nothing to do with whether a particular war is justified or whether isolated incidents in a soldier's war were right or wrong. The point is that war as a human enterprise is a matter of sin. It is a form of hatred for one's fellow human beings. It produces alienation from others and nihilism, and it ultimately represents a turning away from God."[4]

The teenage soldiers do not plan or organize the war. They do not seek to justify it or explain its causes. They are taught, in school, in worship, at home, by the shows they watch and the papers they read, to meld the rhetoric of the state with the rhetoric of religion. They are taught to believe. The symbols of the nation and religion are indistinguishable. The will of God becomes the will of the nation. This belief is shattered in war. Soldiers in combat see the myth used to send them to war implode. They see that war is not clean or neat or noble, but venal, frightening and terrible. They see into war's essence, which is death. They see what is done to others in our name.

War is always about betrayal. The institutions, including religious institutions, that mold us into compliant citizens can never again be trusted by those who return. This betrayal is so deep that many never find their way back to religious faith. They nurse a self-destructive anger and resentment, understandable, but also crippling. Ask a combat veteran struggling to piece his life together about God and watch the raw vitriol spew out of his lips, an anger that pours from him like a cascading torrent. It is this betrayal that creates the chasm between those who have been to war and those who have not. If those who return from war are honest with themselves and others about what they saw and did, and not all are, they can never again embrace this civic religion.

Troops that battle elusive insurgent forces are placed in what the psychiatrist Robert Jay Lifton calls "atrocity producing situations." In this environment, where troops are surrounded by a hostile population, simple acts such as going to a store can be dangerous. The fear and stress leave troops viewing everyone around them as the enemy. When the enemy is shadowy and hard to find, the troops begin to project blame for attacks on civilians. The rage soldiers feel after a roadside bomb explodes, killing their comrades, is one that is easily directed, Lifton argues, to civilians who may support the insurgents. It is a short psychological leap, but a massive moral leap. It is a leap from killing to murder. And in wars such as Vietnam, Iraq, or the Israeli occupation of the West Bank and Gaza, murder dominates the battlefield.

"Ordinary men," Lifton told me one afternoon in Manhattan, "can all too readily be socialized to atrocity. These killing projects are never described as such. They are put in terms of the necessity of improving the world, of political and spiritual renewal. You cannot kill large numbers of people without a claim to virtue. Our own campaign to rid the world of terror is expressed this way, as if once we destroy all terrorists we destroy evil."

War, especially modern warfare, means the razing of villages, the aerial bombing of towns, the deadly toll, long after the war has ended, of land mines strewn about the countryside, and the spread of disease, poverty and birth defects caused by the poisons and destruction left behind. The local population, viewed as a base of support for armed insurgents, is a target. The emotional cost is debilitating

Bishop Packard confronted a crisis of faith. The God he knew, or thought he knew, failed him. He struggled with the capacity we all have for atrocity, with the evil carried out in the name of abstract ideals such as freedom and democracy. Tens of thousands of returning Vietnam veterans were burdened by this betrayal. They turned their backs on organized religion. They had been misled by religious leaders.

Bishop Packard served as a parish priest for two years after he graduated from Virginia Theological Seminary. He became an army chaplain in 1977, he said, "to redeem my experience in the army." He said he grew up believing in "good behavior, in noble service and patriotism," values that endured despite the war. But he wanted to carry out this service another way, his faith no longer rooted in the myth. Three years ago, he became the Episcopal Church's bishop to the armed forces.

"It seemed logical," said Bishop Packard. "I had the deepest experience anyone could have in the military. I can communicate with those facing these ambiguities. Soldiers seem to feel great comfort in my presence. I wanted to give the sacraments to soldiers, to give them strength to face the requirements of being a soldier."

The struggle is always there, rising and falling with life's daily tribulations. Bishop Packard said he is sustained by the power of the liturgy, the scriptural passages that the faithful read each day. In the liturgy he confronts not only his guilt, his repentance, his atonement, but his acceptance of himself as a sinful human being in need of God.

Therapy, for those who have been to war, has limits. The verbal expression of trauma can mitigate the power of awful memories and the delayed stress of combat. It can battle the repression and distrust that make it hard to connect with others, hard to receive or give love. But it is only through the active reformation of a life that guilt and remorse are confronted. Therapists are not always capable of coping with sin. Sin is separation from one's self, one's community and from God. And the only way to overcome this sin is to reconnect by living in another way, by learning how to repent.

Repentance means a turning away from darkness to light. We must name and accept our sin, understand that it remains within us, and use it as a spur to another kind of existence. The bishop became an agent of healing to cope with his wounds. By reaching out to affirm and protect life, his own own life was restored.

Rage, depression and guilt, if left untended or repressed, destroy us. It has to be redirected outward. It has to be the engine that leads to the affirmation that comes through compassion and love. Those who have been to war must shed the outer shells, the hard casings they erect to bury pain and guilt, and find the courage to be vulnerable. They must use the darkness within them to propel them into the light, to carry out acts to heal the wounds they inflicted on themselves and atone for what they inflicted on others. Out of their torment and darkness they can recover.

"The liturgy communicates the presence of God," the bishop said. "And it is this presence that endures beyond the trauma of war. When I read the liturgy to the soldiers I want them to feel the promise of hope and the reconciliation even in the midst of the terror they may face."

The bishop said that after the war he was "unapproachable, angry and distant." It took a toll on his wife and two daughters. He was divorced in 1997, after 28 years of marriage, in large part because of unresolved issues from the war. In 1999 he married Brook, a single mother, and they have a young daughter, Clara. He said he speaks little to Clara about the war, but it comes out in "curiosities," like his discomfort crossing bridges.

The weight of what he did grew harder to bear as he grew older, especially when he began to take part in a church program a decade ago to give food to the homeless in Manhattan.

"It brought back the memories of searching for bodies in the darkness," he said. "But this time it was to give life. It was redemption. I had to face the pain. It was like trying to reconnect pieces of broken wire in the darkness."

He had repetitive nightmares.

"I had killed someone" he said. "No one knew about it. I was trying to hide my crime. I buried the body in a pile of leaves. I was terrified I would be caught."

He stopped and looked somewhere far beyond the walls of his small living room in Rye, New York, that has been his home since 1996.

"Night is the worst," he said slowly. "Nearly all the ambushes I carried out in Vietnam were at night."

He started therapy, something he did for the next eight years, but it was his belief in the power of redemption and forgiveness that rescued him.

"You get wrapped in cellophane so you can function in this world of war," he said. "Only much later, long after you come out, something pricks that cellophane and it all comes out. Then you pray. You pray, 'Lord, forgive me for what I have done.' And you pray to get out of this."

His anger prevented him for years from dealing with his violation of the commandment.

"A few years ago I could not have spoken about it," he said. "I needed to cough up the bile. My deepest sentiments were blocked by anger. I needed to integrate it all, to let it out, to learn to think and feel another way. I needed to understand what happened to me."

This is not what he envisioned as a young man. He did not think this commandment would dominate his life. He did not ask to be betrayed. He did his duty as a patriot and a citizen. He went to war. He came home. He took life. He seeks now to give it.

"When my life is all over," he said, "when in those last 30 seconds that I am fighting for breath in some room, I will make a plea to God. I will say that I did the best I could in the oddities life gave me. I will ask to be forgiven."

ADULTERY

You shall not commit adultery.

If there is one word that defines H. R. Vargas's life, it is rage. If there is one word he would like to define his life, it is love. But loving, and being loved, is not easy for him. The walls went up early when his mother became pregnant and his father walked away. He was taken away from his mother, who beat him and was addicted to drugs. He lived in a series of foster homes, some of which saw him sexually and physically abused. By the time he was a young man he sought love and acceptance in the wrong places, in street gangs, in abusive relationships of his own, in power and even violence.

His father was in a relationship with another woman when he was born. Vargas would not meet him for 21 years. The word "father" is still hard for him to utter, even as he raises two sons of his own. Vargas, known to his friends as Spirit, wears the broken commandment like a heavy chain around his neck. He says it has devastated his life.

"When you commit adultery, you break a promise," he says, "not only to the woman you are in a committed relationship with, not only to the woman you had an affair with, but maybe most important to the children born from the affair.

"My pops was never a father to me. He broke his promise to me on the day I was born. I paid for that broken promise hard, real hard."

We live in an adulterous age. We live in an age when promises and faithfulness, the hard work of fidelity, to values, to the moral life, seem secondary to the drive to attain fleeting scraps of pleasure. Adultery is often viewed as a secondary sin. Vargas's father did not commit adultery in the strict legal interpretation of adultery. He was not married to the woman he was living with when he had his affair. But the consequences of adultery, to the lovers, or to those born from the union, are often disastrous, and from the Bible to the works of Shakespeare and Tolstoy, there is a consistent warning against this particular form of deception, a deception that plays with the deepest, most intimate connections of humankind. Adulterers are thrust into a life of deceit. Children born of the affairs, can grow up with feelings of rejection and inadequacy. Lies, as any affair goes on, pile one on top of the other. It is morally corrosive.

And yet these impulses exist within all of us. No matter how hard we may try to resist the pull of attractive men and women, the promise of excitement, maybe even of fulfillment, holds out the possibility of satisfaction in unsatisfactory lives. Our urges can overpower our mind and our heart. We are unsteady, tipped off balance. We act impulsively, throwing us at first into a frenzy of excitement and then into a free fall until the object of desire becomes tawdry, stale and even repugnant. It is not what we want, after all, not what we are really seeking. The allure of adultery is that it kindles passions that routine and familiarity can leave blunted. This allure is the staple of the advertising and entertainment industries. It is fed to us in a steady stream that flows into our computer terminals, television sets, looks out at us from glossy magazine pages and billboards. The deep destructive power of sexual attraction, the central theme in Greek myth, is a preoccupation of the biblical authors.

Love is the most powerful force in human existence. It allows two people to combine feelings, impulses and wishes that are focused on each other, on the beloved. It allows couples, often with different strengths and weaknesses, to become, through the other, better people, people who bolster strengths and check failings. There is in this love a union that creates a new way of being, a new identity. And this love brings the lovers the life-affirming force of the divine, giving them a way to resist the powerful self-destruction forces that entice us in comparable intensity.

But love is also difficult and hard. It requires us to become vulnerable, to accept self-criticism, to put the needs of another before our own. There is a constant struggle to fine-tune any relationship, to right the slights and wrongs that wound, to take the time for compassion and care. But only in love does the carnal become transcendent.

The desire for an all-consuming love is the most powerful longing in the human heart. There are cultures and societies that try to suppress this longing, often harshly, but it endures. It exists underground, on the margins, struggling against dark forces that see it, rightly, as a threat. The frustration of the strictest mullahs in Iran or the clerics in Afghanistan is the frustration of those who cannot thwart and control love.

Love is at once overwhelming yet fragile, a contradiction that brings together the mind and body, a strange, wondrous force. Religious writers across cultures seek to explain the divine in the language of love. Love is the only force powerful enough to pull us away from idolatry. Societies that plunge themselves into war, or societies that seek to build a state that controls every aspect of human life and thought, work to snuff out the delicacy and tenderness of love, branding it weak and effeminate. A culture that urges us to grasp at momentary bits of pleasure, to indulge in sensuality for its own sake, encourages us to believe that nothing matters. It fosters a culture of self-worship, one that turns us away from the self-denial essential to love. We become entranced with the human mind, with ourselves, even as we create ways for us to perish in a nuclear holocaust, sink under the weight of environmental catastrophe, and build weapons systems that have, in the last century alone, left tens of millions of people dead. Logic and science and technology allow us to believe we control life, to play God. They allow us to manipulate the world for our own ends, even as this manipulation leads to widespread death. When we worship human achievement or the attainment of pleasure as a final end, we live a life dedicated to the self. Love is about the capacity to subsume ourselves for others.

We live in a culture fascinated with stars and celebrities. We are exhorted to stand out from the crowd, to have others admire and envy us, to make a name for ourselves. But this admiration, which is really self-admiration, is one that crowds out the possibility of love, for love places the beloved foremost in life, it sees us make sacrifices for the happiness of the beloved, sacrifices that dent ambition and stunt careers, sacrifices that say there are others more important than ourselves—those we love. For love means that our deepest source of happiness comes in bringing happiness to the beloved. This is a radical way of living, one in stark contradiction to the siren call of self-satisfaction, one that defies the call to live for self. It is the bulwark against the destructive power of those who, angered and alone, seek through power to destroy life. It stymies blind ambition and greed. It creates another way of being.

Love cannot be earned or willed. It is beyond comprehension or control. It is overpowering in its beauty and filled with a transformative power. This is what makes Charles Dickens's *A Christmas Carol,* however sentimental and unsophisticated, a religious work. It chronicles the transformative power of love in a man who worshipped himself. Fidelity to love allows us to reach the highest pinnacle of life. It allows us, even amid sorrow—for when we love deeply we suffer deeply—to live.

The Rev. Gardner C. Taylor wrote:

The greatest things in life are not reasonable. The mind may make sensible comments about these greatest things in life, but they are not reasonable. The love of a mother for her child has reasons, but it is not reasonable. The love of a man for a woman, and the other way around, is surely not reasonable. Beauty, a sunset, the great plunging torrents of Niagara, the final tremendous thunders of the "Hallelujahs" in Handel's Messiah, *the catch in the throat when the sun sets over the sea striking a line of gold on the calm waters touch us at a different level from logic and reason.*

And the love of God for us is not reasonable.[1]

In wartime the culture of death becomes most visible. The intoxication of comradeship works to blot out all love, affection and tenderness. All rhetoric, all posturing, all action seeks to deny the possibility of love.

There is a long sustained assault against the forces of love. Sexual relations in wartime are designed to be carnal, even brutal. Love is seen as sapping the dedication of warriors or those who must endure privations and hardships to build the new society or save the old one. Families are ripped apart. Children are separated from mothers and fathers. People are turned into faceless, nameless numbers on a battlefield, left to die alone, used for misguided or grand schemes of conquest or occupation. The rape of women and girls, as well as the proliferation of pornography and abuse, are intimately linked in war, for all human beings become objects in wartime to eliminate or use for self-gratification. And in such a nihilistic world, where the moral universe has been eclipsed, adultery, like any fleeting pleasure, becomes another diversion, as meaningless as life.

Sebastian Haffner, who was a young lawyer in Berlin when the Nazis took power, wrote of this battle against love in *Defying Hitler*.

The most important part of individual life, which cannot be subsumed in communal life, is love. So comradeship has its special weapon against love: smut. Every evening in bed, after the last patrol round, there was the ritual

reciting of lewd songs and jokes. That is a hard and fast rule of male com-
radeship, and nothing is more mistaken than the widely held opinion that
this is a safety valve for frustrated erotic or sexual feelings. These songs and
jokes do not have an erotic, arousing effect. On the contrary, they make the
act of love appear as unappetizing as possible. They treat it like digestion
and defecation, and make it an object of ridicule. The men who recited rude
songs and used coarse words for female body parts were in effect denying
that they had ever had tender feelings or been in love, that they had ever
made themselves attractive, behaved gently, and used sweet words . . .[2]

Sigmund Freud, although he believed that love was a way to heal
the narcissistic wounds left over from childhood, also acknowledged that there were finally enigmatic, unexplained and mysterious features about being in love. This ineffable quality of love is
one that defeated Freud, along with most who work in the social
sciences. They often seem unable to take on the most important
of human expressions. Love has more commonly been the do-
main of poets, writers, musicians, artists, philosophers and theologians. It defeats those who are not willing to acknowledge that
at its core is wonder and mystery.

The power of love is a concept that is central to most religions, from the Hindu's belief that fullness is only achieved
through the union with the beloved to Plato's discussion of our
search for our other half. Love expands our self. It gives a
wholeness that is lacking in solitary life. It gives us balance. And
sexual relations, rather than an end in itself, becomes the expression of the power and mystery of love, an expression of what
lies beyond articulation, an expression of the eternal, of God.
The loss of love, either through abandonment or deception or
death, is one that plunges us into despair so profound that its
consequences can often mean spiritual and sometimes physical
death. Adultery, at its core, means unfaithfulness to the beloved,
even if that beloved is the partner in the adulterous affair. And

this unfaithfulness is one that, as no shortage of poets and writers have told us through the ages, can eventually see us destroy that which is sacred, love itself.

Love is not benign. It is a threat to those in power, to movements that demand self-sacrifice, to those who wage war, to the very core of the civic religion every state seeks to build out of its prevailing religious tradition. It is as much a threat to those who recruit suicide bombers as it is a threat to those who direct the war in Iraq. For love defies the conventions of duty. It subverts the goals of the state. It leads us to reject false covenants. Religious leaders, from Moses to Buddha to Christ to Mohammed, know how dangerous love is to those who seek and hold temporal power. The core of nearly all religious teaching is about love and compassion, compassion for those we love and for our neighbors, but also for the world around us and even for those who hate us. It is about pushing this love outward into the world. This compassion, which does not exclude justice, is one that urges us to have empathy for the other, to stand in the other's shoes. It is the first prerequisite to making peace, to healing personal and national conflict and to defying the powers on earth that drive us to serve other gods. The forces that seek to harness the power of religion and deform it into a civic religion have no use for the fundamental core call to love. Indeed, it is the message they seek most actively to destroy, even as they cloak themselves in religious piety and employ religious language.

Love is always driven underground in states ruthlessly bent on achieving power and expanding empire. It is why Aeneas in Virgil's *The Aeneid* abandoned his lover Dido, the queen of Carthage, to found Rome. But his noble cause led Dido to commit suicide and left Aeneas in despair.

When Krzysztof Kieslowski filmed his story on adultery he centered it on a woman who was not married. He understood that the commandment was not simply about about the bonds of marriage, for vows are often broken or left unfulfilled, but the danger of relationships not built on love.

The film opens with 19-year-old Tomek training his telescope from his bedroom window on the apartment across the court-yard. Through the lens of the telescope we see a beautiful, older woman, Magda, undressing. Tomek watches her night after night, but he turns his telescope away when she takes a new sexual part-ner to bed. It is too much for him to bear. He eventually meets her and confesses his love. She has sex with the inexperienced boy, and then belittles his inadequacy. He flees home and slits his wrists. The film follows his physical, if not emotional, recovery. It portrays her guilt and desire to have him back, to have a love that goes beyond the carnal. But love is crushed for the young man.

The rage that consumes Vargas is a rage born out of a life without love, a life conceived outside of romantic love, a life where he was forced to live alone. And this rage, the rage of the unloved, pushes Vargas to destroy as he has been destroyed. This barren universe can leave emotions dead and numb. Abuse and violence is possible against the innocent and the weak. Those de-nied love often become agents for love's obliteration.

We know something of this rage. When we are rejected, or be-trayed by those we love, those we have opened ourselves to be in-timate with, we taste a bit of death, the ultimate rejection of our being. Rejection, especially as profound a rejection as Vargas en-dured, diminishes and destroys us. The only hope of renewal is forgiveness. If we cannot forgive, if we cannot allow ourselves to be vulnerable again, we shut out the possibility of friendship and love. And once this door is closed we become, in some sense, dead. We die, like orphans that are not held and coddled as in-fants, without love. It is as vital as water.

In *The Origins of Totalitarianism,* a study of the rise of the totali-tarian states in Nazi Germany and the Soviet Union, Hannah Arendt calls these solitary unloved figures "atomized individuals."

She argues that a life without love is not only the curse of modernity, but one of the primary reasons totalitarian movements can recruit so many followers. These followers seek in the state or the party the love and intimacy they have been denied in their personal lives. The state sanctifies their rage. Violence fills up the emotional void. They mistake comrades for family. Vargas was drawn to the street gang, the Latin Kings, for similar reasons. But the gang, with its violence and drug dealing, manipulated his longing to be loved. As Arendt wrote:

> *What prepares men for totalitarian domination in the non-totalitarian world is the fact that loneliness, once a borderline experience usually suffered in certain marginal social conditions like old age, has become an everyday experience of the evergrowing masses of our century. The merciless process into which totalitarianism drives and organizes the masses looks like a suicidal escape from this reality. The "ice-cold reasoning" and the "mighty tentacle" of dialectics which "seizes you as in a vise" appears like a last support in a world where nobody is reliable and nothing can be relied upon.*[3]

Vargas, now into adulthood, was visiting his half brother recently in the Bronx. His half brother told him that the older man in a chair in the living room was "our father." Vargas recoiled, angered that "father" had been the word used to describe the stranger in front of him.

His father, who never lived with his mother and made no effort to contact him, felt equally insulted, Vargas said, when he did not follow the traditional Puerto Rican custom of asking his father for a blessing.

"I blew up," says Vargas, recalling his father's reaction. "I asked him where he had been all my life. I told him he was never a father to me. He could not demand anything from me. I told him to go to hell."

At age four, Vargas along with his brother and his sister, was taken from his mother. They were placed in different foster homes. The move, which separated him for the rest of his life from his brother and sister, was at first fortunate. Living with his foster mother Lucy, who raised him for the next four years, was the only stable time of his life. He refers to Lucy as "the mother I never had."

But at age eight he was sent back to his mother. The return, which severed him forever from Lucy, thrust him again into a world of despair and loneliness.

"When my biological mother came to get me I ran to Lucy and held her and did not let go," he says. "Lucy went to court to try and get me back, but they never gave me back to her."

He spent six months with his mother, months when he was again abused and beaten. He was sent to another foster home. He was shuttled from home to home, staying at some for only a few days. He withdrew, nursing a childhood anger that would blossom into violent crime, a loss of touch with his own feelings and volcanic outbursts. He never felt like celebrating his birthdays.

As the child of an adulterous relationship, he said he learned not to trust, not to feel and to always expect the worst. He was sexually and physically abused in several foster homes. "There are days I walk through the Bronx and dream about meeting the son in one foster family who abused me," he says. "I only remember his face. I don't care how established I am in life. I will kill him."

Vargas dropped out of high school. He joined the Latin Kings and "graduated into a thug." He began to sell heroin. At first, membership in the gang seemed to answer the longings he had for affection, but he found the camaraderie on the street was ultimately hollow.

"When I first joined the nation," Vargas says, speaking of the gang, "people would call me brother. They said that when any of us were touched we were all touched. I felt powerful for the first time. It felt like love."

He made several hundred dollars a day selling drugs. He went to fancy restaurants in Manhattan where he could "eat where the white folks eat." He was arrested on weapons charges when he was 16 and sent to Rikers Island. He ended up in the adult wing, a bureaucratic mistake that led to his being released early. Several of the older prisoners, in a kind of love, told him to straighten out and start over.

"People change in jail," Vargas says. "The real person comes out. It is different from the streets. There were men in there who were never going to get out. They told me not to end up like them. I learned a different way to be. It sounds soft, but it brought out a stronger side."

He returned to the street in 1994 and told his drug employers he was finished. He could not afford a place to stay and slept in homeless shelters or Covenant House, a nonprofit residence for homeless youths. He found a girlfriend, Marilyn Rodriguez. They had his first child, Raziel.

"It was scary," he says. "I looked at my son and knew I did not know how to be a father. No one had been there to teach me. I did not know how to love. I only knew what I had seen on soap operas. I did not understand love. It is still new to me."

Life is a battle to rip down the barriers and manage the rage that torments him. He often fails. He blames himself, even for his rejection, wondering if he is worthy of love. He knows that he does things that should be rejected. He has been physically abusive to those he loves. He seeks atonement for this. He knows that some of him, these fragments of him, should be rejected, but he fears that in this rejection can come a rejection of who he is, who he wants to become. This frightens him.

"The hardest thing is to talk about my feelings," he says. "I am not the type of person to give someone a hug, although now I try to be. I am afraid to let people know who I really am, to see the kind of person I am. My character might show that I am a thug, but inside I am not my image."

He and Marilyn had twins a year before I met Vargas, but after two months one of them, Ryan Sebastian, died from kidney failure.

"Ryan died in my arms," he says. "I had to bury him. I left the cemetery in rage. I had been a little boy who never had a father or a mother. I had been raped and beaten as a child over and over and over. I was in prison. I was homeless. And all that was nothing compared to losing my son."

He blamed the surviving twin, Bryan Christopher, for Ryan's death. He could not be affectionate with Bryan for months.

"It was a long time before I could accept that Ryan's death was not Bryan's fault," Vargas says. "I had to learn to see Ryan in Bryan."

Marilyn, after an argument, left him and the boys. She came back, but the arguments continued. She left again. He fumbles to be a father, to keep a promise that was never kept for him, to hold on to his relationships, to find love, to conquer rage.

"When you say you will marry someone, then you tell them you will love them no matter what," he says. "They have permission to hurt you and you are still supposed to love them. Now I am asking if love has any limitations."

He stands in his living room in front of a huge television screen holding Bryan, his beefy tattooed forearm saying "Marilyn forgive me for I have sinned" wrapped around the small child.

"I beat her," he says of the tattoo, "and got this to say I am sorry."

On his back is a tattoo of the Grim Reaper. On his left upper arm is a heart with the names of Marilyn and Justin, her son from another relationship.

Not long ago he decided to find Lucy. He drove to Red Hook in Brooklyn where she lived and rang every doorbell on the block until a man who said he was Lucy's son answered the door.

"Yo," he told the man, "I am here to see Ma."

The son told him Lucy was dead. His rage ignited like the explosion of a blast furnace. He got in his car and sped down the highway. It did not matter if he crashed. Nothing mattered.

"I left real angry," he says. "I was so upset at her for dying."

Vargas fights to hang on as a husband and a father, roles that were absent in his life. There are days when it seems strange and unfamiliar.

"I need to break down the patterns I had before," he says. "I need love. I am like a small child that makes a lot of mistakes. People have to be patient with me. I have no experience with this. I never had a father. No one wanted me for a son."

—•—

THEFT

You shall not steal.

When R. Foster Winans got out of prison he was sent to a halfway house in Times Square in New York. Most of those in the halfway house were devoting their energy to resisting the temptations of crack dealers. The dreary, run-down brownstone was next to *The New York Times* on West 43rd Street. A transvestite bar was across the street.

In the morning Winans walked outside and looked at the flags hanging over the revolving door of the newspaper.

"I had written pieces for *The New York Times* before I went to *The Wall Street Journal,*" says the former journalist. "It was a daily reminder how low I had sunk. My career was finished. I was surrounded by people who had no interest in rehabilitation. Many of my friends had died of AIDS. New York was a place of ghosts."

In 1983 Winans, then 35, was cowriting the "Heard on the Street" column for *The Wall Street Journal,* one of the best-read stock market columns in the country. If a company was praised in the column the price of its stock often rose the next day. If a company was disparaged its share price often dipped. He was making $28,000 a year and went home to a small apartment on a block of six-story tenements on East 14th Street, but for a man who had never completed college and grown up in rural Pennsylvania his job, which he loved, represented success.

He wrote about the deals orchestrated by financial power brokers who were raking in millions, often in ways that were unethical and unlawful. He watched the feeding frenzy in Wall Street from behind the glass partitions of his profession. He saw those making money dine in the city's finest restaurants, navigate through traffic in limousines, fuel their long workdays with cocaine and flaunt the tailored suits, homes and vacations that come with massive wealth. The world he wrote about glittered before his eyes. It was alluring, unreachable and seductive. He resented the ease of their lives, while he struggled to pay rent. He wanted more.

It looked easy enough. Insider trading was rife, fueled by a buoyant market and huge mergers that handed the fate of corporations to investment bankers. Those on the inside took care of themselves, passing on private, vital investment information and cutting deals behind closed doors before mergers went public or earnings reports were released. This gave them, and the wealthy clients they worked for, an advantage in stock trades and huge profits. Stock research analysts, who are supposed to impartially rate stocks for investors, instead lauded stocks from corporations that were paying huge banking fees to their firms. These analysts were also being highly compensated for bringing in new business, although the conflicts of interest were never disclosed to millions of investors, who relied on the analysts being interviewed on television or quoted in columns such as the one written by Winans. Independent auditors, to cover up the theft, were put on the payroll of the corporations they were hired to monitor. When Enron went bankrupt it was paying Arthur Andersen a million dollars a week in consulting fees, although the accounting firm was also in charge of carrying out independent audits on Enron for investors.[1] The internal accounting within corporations became an elaborate shell game, with reports of phantom profits and hidden losses. Corporations stopped reporting stock options, although they meant diverting millions to its top executives, as expenses in their earnings reports.

The rampant corruption and corporate theft saw millions of Americans lose their retirement savings and money put aside for their children's education. The accounting industry, stock analysts, regulatory agencies, investment bankers and the heads of the country's corporations robbed the public. The country's tiny oligarchy amassed huge fortunes. Between 1989 and 1997, 86 percent of stock market gains went to the top 10 percent of American households.[2]

"Research analysts were just the pawnbrokers for a much larger scam," Winans says. "Trading desks at major brokerage houses, where the real money is made, harvested and exploited insider information about analysts' recommendations to reward their most profitable accounts, the institutional investors like mutual and pension funds. A subculture sprung up just to cash in on corporate 'whisper numbers,' those salacious-sounding quarterly profit forecasts leaked to analysts before the rest of the investing public. Handouts of sure-thing initial public stock offerings to favored clients have been well documented, but don't expect billion-dollar settlements."

The crimes he saw going on around him were hard for outsiders to detect. There were few prosecutions. The rewards were immense. This deceit was deeply embedded in the investment world. Those who were slick and well connected did not seem to get caught, or if they did, they received little more than a slap on the wrist. Winans grew tired of being the little guy, watching from the sidelines as others exploited the system while he struggled.

"It was like being in a candy store," he says, "and there was nobody behind the counter. You think, who's going to miss a few butterscotches?"

The crime he committed was a small infraction, but a symptom of the deep ethical and moral morass within American culture that began during the Reagan years. The market, Reagan officials argued, could regulate itself. But with no checks or watchdog agencies left, greed soon began to assume unheard-of proportions. CEOs of companies helped themselves to hundreds of millions of dollars as their small investors were wiped out. Nearly all of the top Enron executives, despite amassing fortunes in the hundreds of millions of dollars, have avoided prison or huge fines.

Those who played by the rules lost. Those who didn't got rich.

"That leads to cynicism and undermines legitimacy in the system," Winans says. "In that environment, why not make up your own rules?"

Winans was on Wall Street at the start of this era of deregulation, astronomical profits, expanding markets and widespread corporate crime, crime that has since cost taxpayers hundreds of billions of dollars. The numbers are dizzying. Health care fraud alone is estimated at $100 billion to $400 billion a year.[3] The savings and loan fraud of the late 1980s—which former attorney general Dick Thornburgh called "the biggest white collar swindle in history"—cost the country anywhere from $300 billion to $500 billion.[4] And corporations that commit massive fraud are rarely punished.

America's new oligarchy is creating a world that resembles the one shaped by the robber barons of the last century, a world where workers struggle on inadequate salaries without job protection or health care and the rich create private kingdoms of wealth and privilege. This growing disparity in wealth sees the top 1 percent of households wealthier than the entire bottom 90 percent combined.[5]

This oligarchy has fused political and economic power. It funds and controls the two main political parties, leaving the working class without representation. There are an estimated 40 lobbyists for every member of Congress and these lobbyists spend over $1.5 billion a year[6] on behalf of their powerful clients to abolish restrictions on monopolies, further weaken regulatory agencies, roll back environmental protection and push through greater tax breaks for the wealthy and their corporate interests.

There is a revolving door between the corporate world and government. After Dick Cheney left the first Bush administration, where he was secretary of defense, he became the CEO of Halliburton, the largest oil services company in the world. He was paid a salary of $60 million for the five years he worked there. During his tenure he obtained almost $2 billion in tax-payer-insured loans from the Export-Import Bank of the United States and the Overseas Private Investment Corporation. In addition, he secured $2.3 billion in government contracts.[7] The company was also accused of inflating profits by $234 million, something that produced over a dozen lawsuits for "accounting irregularities."[8] These inflated earnings reports are common within corporations that use them to ensure a steady stream of investors and hike up stock options for company executives.

And when Cheney stepped back into a position of power, his friends reaped the benefits. The war in Iraq has been a boon for defense and oil corporations, with an estimated third of the $4 billion monthly cost of the Iraq occupation being paid out to private contractors such as Halliburton, the largest government contractor in Iraq.[9] Private security firms have mounted a rogue army of some 20,000 mercenaries, who lie beyond the reach of the military or the law. And President Bush in May 2003 signed an executive order that allows oil companies immunity against contractual disputes or lawsuits resulting from discrimination, labor law abuses, environmental disasters and human rights violations.[10] The oil companies in Iraq are, in essence, beyond the reach of the law and can seize and exploit Iraqi resources without regard to the rights of Iraqis.[11]

When government and public institutions are no longer

trusted, when they become engines solely for personal power and wealth at the expense of the interests and welfare of the public, it sends the message that honesty does not pay. There is a loss of faith in the structures designed to hold community together. Trust evaporates. People begin to believe nothing, or rather, they believe what they want to believe. Established media organs relay the lies of the powerful with little or no scrutiny, serving to further obscure the truth. A society without the means to detect lies and theft soon squanders its liberty and freedom.

This erosion of public trust, as Hannah Arendt wrote, leaves us increasingly open to dangerous manipulation by the enemies of open societies, those who disdain democracy as inherently weak and inefficient.

> *It has frequently been noticed that the surest long-term result of brainwashing is a peculiar kind of cynicism—an absolute refusal to believe in the truth of anything, no matter how well this truth may be established. In other words, the result of a consistent and total substitution of lies for factual truth is not that the lies will now be accepted as truth, and the truth be defamed as lies, but that the sense by which we take our bearings in the real world—and the category of truth vs. falsehood is among the mental means to this end—is being destroyed.*[12]

Winans insists he did not manipulate or mislead readers, rather he failed to disclose a conflict of interest. But his violation was part of a growing violation of the trust between many in the media conglomerates and their readers, listeners and viewers. This trust is the foundation of a free press and an open society. The reader trusts the reporter not to manipulate or distort information, not to intentionally mislead or lie. The reporter writes the truth, even if this is a truth the reporter finds uncomfortable or the reader does not want to hear. By using his column for personal gain, by taking advantage of his knowledge of the paper's content before it was published, he betrayed this contract with the reader. This betrayal has spawned hundreds of impersonators in the profession of journalism. Television personalities, who rarely if ever actually report a story, dish out news as entertainment. They feed us chatter and spin that no longer seeks to serve the public but to boost their own ratings, whip up self-congratulatory feelings of patriotism and power and increase advertising revenue. They are infected with the cynicism that destroyed Winans's career and scuttled his integrity. The *Los Angeles Times* editor John S. Carroll calls these armies of imposters "pseudo-journalists."

"All across America," Carroll said, "there are offices that resemble newsrooms, and in those offices there are people who resemble journalists, but they are not engaged in journalism. It is not journalism because it does not regard the reader—or, in the case of broadcasting, the listener, or the viewer—as a master to be served.

"To the contrary, it regards its audience with a cold cynicism. In this realm of pseudo-journalism, the audience is something to be manipulated. And when the audience is misled, no one in the pseudo-newsroom ever offers a peep of protest."[13]

Rhetoric no longer has any link with reality. Politicians announce that the corrupt will be punished, yet they remain untouched. Politicians say the war in Iraq is making us safer, yet it ignites a worldwide rage against us. Spin, the intentional effort to distort information for political gain, is a respected asset in every political camp.

The disconnection between what is said and what is real has led huge numbers of voters to check out of the system. They feel abandoned by the Democrats and Republicans. The loss of manufacturing jobs has left millions of American workers adrift, knocked off balance, battling despair and apathy, searching desperately for another way to make a living. The industrial flight has spawned depressed and impoverished factory towns, including my family's former mill town in Maine. The working class has been tossed into the ranks of the poor. They eke out a living, at best, on minimum wage at Wal-Marts or in the service industry, part of 45 million Americans without health care or retirement benefits.

Despair has given way to rage. It is a rage fueled by trash talk radio shows, television evangelists and others who promise revenge. The rage is augmented by fear, by the strange and blood-curdling calls by Islamic terrorists for America's destruction and the threat of future terrorism. In the hands of demagogues, this rage has been turned on minorities, feminists, liberals and gays and lesbians.

The desperation is dangerous. The nationalist wars in Yugoslavia were presaged by a similar economic meltdown, as was the rise of the 20th century's most frightening totalitarian movements in Germany and Russia. The corporate theft that swept up Winans was part of this assault against the nation's working class and the values that make liberty possible. The victimless white-collar crime that Winans thought would hurt no one threatens, especially if we suffer more terrorist attacks, to contribute to the erosion of our democracy.

The largest corporations, based outside the United States, beyond the reach of the law or tax authorities, have built an unholy alliance with Washington to prop up repressive regimes. The rulers in countries such as Nigeria live off kickbacks from corporations such as Chevron. These rulers do not hinder corporate profits or impede the exploitation of natural resources. The president of the Congo in Brazzaville told me a few years ago he did not know how much the French oil giant Elf was taking out of his country. The puppet regimes suppress the press, crush labor movements and make a farce of democratic elections. The role of American corporations, who have long bullied and manipulated states in Africa and Latin America, is antidemocratic. This is what they do abroad. Now they have begun to do it at home.

But Winans, like most of us, saw none of this. He was focused on himself, his own wants, his own resentments, especially when set against the lavish world in front of him. He was not interested in questioning. The object was to get in on the winnings, even if that meant theft and betrayal. He was blind to the consequences.

He developed a friendship with a multimillionaire stockbroker named Peter N. Brant. Brant was one of the richest and most successful retail brokers on Wall Street. He had a corner office at Kidder, Peabody & Co.'s branch on Park Avenue, a large house on Long Island's exclusive North Shore, a membership at the New York Racquet Club, a condo in Palm Beach and a closet of fine silk suits. He commuted to work in a helicopter, owned horses and played polo.

Brant had changed his name from Bornstein to Brant in an apparent effort to cultivate the image of old Wasp money. He was aggressive, his commission revenue was high and the firm's executives held him up as a model. He worked the right circles, inspired confidence and attracted big money.

His empire, however, was in trouble. He had invested heavily in technology stocks that were falling. Winan's column offered him a way to recoup his losses.

The two men sat one rainy night in New York at the Racquet Club. Brant suggested they cut a deal. Winans would tell him in advance if a stock was going to be named as a good buy and he would snap up shares before the column appeared in the paper. The two would share the profits from the sale.

"Wouldn't you like to be a millionaire?" he asked Winans.

"Sure," Winans answered.

Brant proposed they make a few million dollars, Winans remembered. Brant said he would then open his own firm. Winans would leave the paper and work for him.

"I never thought of it as a crime," Winans says. "Insider trading was epidemic. It seemed that in one way or another, everyone was exploiting the system. The smell of easy money was in the air.

I was seduced by the scent, but it had less to do with money and more to do with low self-esteem and the desire for attention."

Brant lacked finesse. It did not take long to tie the repeated coincidences between his trades and the newspaper column. The Securities and Exchange Commission called Winans and asked him about the collaboration. His editor listened in on the taped conversation.

"I lied," Winans says. "It is a basic instinct, like fight or flight. And, like fight or flight, it often causes needless grief. When people get into trouble they tend to hide it, but this starts an engine of self-destruction along with conflicted and bad behavior."

He had deposited checks from Brant in his bank account. The paper trail was hard to hide. His lies multiplied and became tangled in a messy web. He sought refuge in vague excuses for two weeks. But every lie sprouted dozens more. It became hard to keep track. When he learned he was under investigation he thought about suicide. He planned his death and then backed down. He confessed to his editors and lost his job. He was charged, although he pleaded not guilty arguing that the law was vague. It was vague enough to see the case brought before the Supreme Court more than two years later, but not vague enough for him to escape conviction. Prosecutors estimated that the scheme netted $675,000, though Winans and his roommate, also a conspirator, shared only $31,000 of the profits. Winans served nine months in a minimum-security federal prison in Danbury, Connecticut.

He moved into prison with some 70 other inmates all sleeping in one room in bunk beds. There was one television. He had to wait in line to make a phone call. All calls, which were limited to 15 minutes, were recorded. Prison was boring, deadening, but also, he says, "the best thing that ever happened to me, although I would not recommend it."

"Many of the men I met in prison did not get there thinking like criminals," he says. "Most started out cutting corners in business, 'borrowing' from the future until they were so enmeshed in fraud there was no fixing what they'd done or putting back what they'd stolen."

He read Viktor Frankl's book *Man's Search for Meaning,* which he says "changed my life." A community, he began to understand, flourished when it trusted its leaders and institutions. It fell apart when it did not. Trust, he learned, required sacrifice, even sacrifice that put you in jeopardy. It required one to think beyond the narrow definition of self-interest and material gain.

"Frankl is in Auschwitz and gives up a chance to escape to take care of a man dying of TB because it was the right thing to do," Winans says. "The prisoner he was planning to escape with was caught and killed. Frankl, by choosing what he thought was death, survived. There is a huge message in this story. There is a secret pleasure in invisibly doing the right thing. When this becomes a habit, your conscience is clear. You are free."

He moved back to Doylestown, Pennsylvania, where he grew up because, he says, "there is integrity in going home."

"I needed authenticity," he says. "This is where I am from. I got disgusted with New York. I looked at other areas, all the pretentious places, such as the north shore of Long Island. I thought I would never come back, but I needed to learn how to live again."

He makes his living ghost writing, and has published about a dozen books, including a popular series of historical novels for young readers. None carry his name.

"The series became very successful, but I was despondent," he says. "I received no fan mail, never did a book signing, never shook the hand of an appreciative reader, never knew how the books were being received. This was the hardest part of clearing my conscience, letting go of my ego and the public payback for my work. But when I did, I felt liberated from a burden."

Winans is sitting at a wrought-iron table at a restaurant in Doylestown with its antique shops, ice cream parlors, boutiques and well-kept white clapboard homes. He drinks wine spritzer, "heavy on the spritzer." He is thin and balding, modestly dressed in dark slacks and a collared shirt.

He tells me of the things he has done since this "unhappy chapter in my life." He started a writer's room in the town for local authors. He nursed a man who was dying of AIDS. These are new stories to define him, to make amends. He wonders if any act can be truly good if others know about it. He is worried about intentions, doing things that appear to be good to bolster an image. He says he is through with images. Images got him into trouble.

He has run up again against the impulse to lie and flee. His 18-year-old nephew, Ben, was living with him. Ben came from a difficult home. He had used drugs as a teenager and been sent away to a teen boot camp. The counselors at the boot camp punished children by bending their hands backward until they screamed or sent them to solitary confinement. Ben fled the boot camp and was homeless until his uncle flew him home.

"He arrived angry and full of attitude," Winans says. "He discussed selling drugs and 'doing dirt.' He looked and acted like a convict, keeping his head shaved, walking with an exaggerated swagger, using prison language. Although he had never been convicted of anything, he was in every other respect an escaped inmate. The police in any state would have had the right to arrest him. They could have sent him back to Utah to wait out the seven months remaining until he turned eighteen and was legally emancipated."

Ben had scratched a crude tattoo on his right forearm with a straight pin and ink from a ballpoint pen. It was his mother's name, Finch. He later had it professionally redone and added his last name to the other forearm. He wore on his arms the family names of his father and mother.

"It was a painful cry for family love," Winans says.

Winans helped him find an apartment and a job at a bagel shop. Ben, however, left for California after five months, to be with a girlfriend. Winans says he greeted the move "with relief." Four months later Ben was back.

He walked in the door one fall night after a trip to New York and shakily told his uncle: "I've got a situation. I think I hurt somebody bad."

He had been standing in front of the Starbucks with a group of teenagers. He needed money for the train into New York when another boy asked if he could sell him some marijuana. Ben wrapped some coins in a piece of foil from a pack of cigarettes. He and the boy walked around the corner into an alley. He intended to scam him in the drug deal. They began to argue about the price. It turned into a fight. Ben hit him. The boy, who would suffer a concussion but recover, fell on the pavement with a thud. Ben grabbed the boy's money and ran to the train station.

Ben was questioned by the police two weeks later. He lied, as had his uncle years before. The police called to make an appointment to question Winans. Winans called his nephew. He informed Ben he would be present during the interview. He told Ben he would have to confess. When the police arrived Ben admitted to the crime. He was convicted and given a year of work release followed by a year on parole.

Winans bearded, intense, carries the burden of his past, of sins forgotten or dismissed as trivial by others, but heavy for him. He collects stories like these, a kind of karma to purge him from his past. He reminds me of Jim in Joseph Conrad's novel *Lord Jim,* out to redeem a wrong others no longer remember.

Winans quotes Martin Luther: "A bad conscience can only make men cowardly and fearful."

He reads books about the death camps, about how people made moral choices in extreme situations. He understands that redemption will not come in one monumental act, but the small acts of daily life, acts that often go unnoticed by others. Moral choice can only be moral because it is right, not because it brings us any benefit.

In Conrad's novel the ramshackle old ship the *Patna,* filled with pilgrims on their way to the Holy Land, hit something below the surface. The officers were the only ones who knew about the disaster. They decided to secretly abandon the ship. Jim, the chief mate, resisted, watching passively as they launched the lifeboat. Jim was disgusted with the cowardice of the crew. But as the life boat was pulling away Jim impulsively leapt to join them. Who would know? The pilgrims, after all, would die. It was this shame of naked fear and self-preservation that would color the rest of his life.

The ship, however, remained afloat and was towed into port by a French gunboat. There was a judicial inquiry. The crew, with the exception of Jim, fled town. Jim alone was tried, found guilty and stripped of his certificate. All life became an effort to cancel out what he did, to find redemption. As Conrad wrote elsewhere, "there is a taint of death, a flavour of mortality in lies. . . ."[14]

Augustine defined a lie as any statement meant to deceive another. No lie, he wrote, is ever justified, for it sets up a dichotomy between what we say and what is in our hearts. It was a position that would later be adopted by Immanuel Kant, not only because the lie harmed others, but because, he argued, it destroyed the liar.[15] A lie not only deceives others, turning them into objects to be manipulated and used, rendering them less than human, but a lie erodes trust, the cement that holds communities and relationships together. Lies lead to cynicism. This cynicism spreads outward like a disease until it blights the landscape.

"By a lie a man throws away and, as it were, annihilates his dignity as a man,"[16] Kant wrote in *Doctrine of Virtue.*

It was his dignity Winans wanted back. He planned to earn it. I wondered if his anguish was matched by those who stole hundreds of millions from Enron shareholders, many living in sprawling ranches in Colorado or penthouses in Houston. I wondered if they had much time for his soul searching. Perhaps they can still think of themselves as winners. By the standards of crass materialism they would be right. Winans is convinced the world will only change one person at a time. It is our behavior that defines our life.

"We've lost, as a culture, the instinct to reach out to others," Winans says. "We think we don't have time, or resources, or we fear making a commitment that will cost us more than we think we have to share. We cannot help everyone, and some people cannot be helped. But that shouldn't stop us from trying. We should give in to those instincts often, in every aspect of life, without calculating the expense or the payoff."

"Redemption is a process," he says. "Redemption suggests that you have learned something in life, that through your example you pass values on to others. Redemption suggests your life has meaning. This meaning is always about sacrifice, about helping others and perhaps about being invisible. Redemption means life is not about me. It means you have to be willing to give up everything, even your life, to be saved. It means resisting the temptation to steal and always telling the truth, even when it hurts you, even when you are afraid. It means having dignity. It means trust."

DECALOGUE IX

———◆———

ENVY

You shall not bear false witness against your neighbor.

In the Far East, where the game of chess was invented around
A.D. 600, stones were placed on each corner of the board to keep
the evil of the match from spilling into the world. But there are
no stones on the boards in the rival chess shops on Thompson
Street in New York City's Greenwich Village. Evil spills out into
the streets.

The owners of the Chess Shop, at 230 Thompson Street, and
the Chess Forum, at 219 Thompson Street, along with the patrons who go to one shop and not the other, are bitter and impla-
cable rivals. The two owners, former partners, have filed lawsuits.
They have had their customers take loyalty oaths. They have ac-
cused the rival of spying and theft. They have engaged in name-
calling and what each side labels character assassination. One
shop briefly barred disloyal patrons. The shops unleash price
wars, hemorrhaging money in the hopes of wiping out the other.
And all those involved, cursed with minds that often see life as
another version of an intricate battle between little pieces of
wood on a board, create whirlpools of intrigue and hatred.

"It does not make very good business sense," admits Imad
Khachan, who owns the Chess Forum. "We would both make
more money if we worked together."

The two shops, within sight of each other, are similar. They are
dominated by tables where players sit, their heads bent over chess
boards, for a dollar an hour. There is soft background music, with
the Chess Shop preferring classical and the Chess Forum light
pop. The players rarely speak. They slam the wooden pieces on
the board with an audible thump. The walls in each shop need a
coat of paint. The bathrooms are grimy. The shelves are stacked
with hundreds of chess sets, from the traditional forms to theme
sets with pieces from *The Simpsons* and *Star Trek*. The shops have
big windows along the street where dozens of sets are on display.
They have more sets in glass cases inside. Prices run from about
$5 for a small magnetic set to $10,000 for a modern bronze set
cast by the artist Mark Pilato.

The Bible warns, from the story of Cain and Abel to the commandment not to bear false witness against your neighbor, of the
destructive power of perpetual war against a rival. Such rivalry
usually ends not only with the destruction of the enemy but self-
destruction. The hatred, eventually, consumes all who embrace it.
On Thompson Street the rivals suffer losses and are consumed by
rage in the frenzied drive to destroy each other. The war between
them is steadily evolving from a calculated effort to annihilate the
other to suicide.

The most insular communities, those whose lives intersect in
worlds and subcultures that exclude outsiders, often seem to suffer the most crippling jealousy and envy. The church and univer-
sities are notorious caldrons of intrigue and slander. Neglect
breeds insecurity and fear of irrelevance. This fear does not tolerate dissenters within the ranks. There is, in such inbred communities, a need to be perceived as holding a pure, unchallenged
orthodoxy. They constantly feel threatened with extinction. They
need to hate. They must direct the venom felt toward an indif-
ferent world onto the only people who would bother to listen or
care, those who are like them.

This chess war is a fratricide. It grew out of apostasy. It began with the worship by a younger follower of an older mentor, a father figure, one who would guide the younger man through life. It ended with feelings of betrayal and abandonment.

But the betrayal had roots in larger betrayals, in betrayals that left millions of disrupted lives and millions of dead. This story began before there were two small chess shops on Thompson Street. It began in Russia in 1917 with the winter revolution that toppled the old order, abolished the ruling class, saw the tsar and his family murdered, and replaced it with the communist order, or what the Yugoslav dissident Milovan Djilas, in his own act of apostasy, would call "the new class."

In 1910 Nicolas Rossolimo, who would go on to become one of the world's greatest chess players, was born in the city of Kiev of a Greek father, a painter, and a Russian mother with ties to the aristocracy. His family, after being confined by the communists in a basement, fled to France in 1919. By 1938 he was one of the best players in Europe, winning the championship of Paris ten times. In 1953, a grand master, he arrived in New York and started the Chess Studio where chess lovers and émigré intellectuals congregated. His shop looked like a down-at-the-heels Russian tea room. He had come to New York at the age of 43. He was ranked 15th in the world, the highest ranking he would ever achieve. He would represent the United States in the chess Olympiads of 1958, 1960 and 1966. But life was hard, and as in Paris, he worked driving a taxi to support his tiny shop, often sleeping amid the playing tables at night.

The Chess Studio was on Sullivan Street in Greenwich Village. It was hard for Rossolimo to make enough to pay the rent, especially given the grand master's love of drink and his constant traveling, including long periods in France. The chaos of another violent upheaval tossed a young German, George Frohlinde, also a lover of chess, into his lap. Frohlinde, who was never to be a great chess player, was unable to find work after the war in Germany as a carpenter. He arrived in 1958 in New York. Frohlinde said he had spent the war playing chess in his local club in Wismar on the Baltic Sea, "watching the fleets of allied bombers pass overhead on the way to bomb Berlin."

He refuses when I meet him to tell his age, but concedes that he is in his 70s. He has long strands of gray hair that fall onto the shoulders of his worn leather jacket. We talk in a small office in the Chess Shop. There is a bare neon light overhead and a brown fly strip, covered with black specks of dead bugs, dangling from the ceiling. He is visiting. His nephew, Laurence Nash, manages the shop. He says he gravitated, like all chess lovers in New York, to Rossolimo's studio, but he had given up on competition by the time the war ended in Germany. "I decided life was bigger than sixty-four squares."

He started working behind the counter in Rossolimo's shop. He checked out the boards to players and managed the inventory. Rossolimo was often away, and by 1963, nostalgic for France, the chess master, who was slipping steadily in the world rankings, moved to Paris. He put his German protégé in charge of the business.

"He wanted to reconnect with his days of glory," Frohlinde says dismissively. "He asked me to take over the shop for a year. We made a funny contract. I got seventy-five percent of the profits and he got twenty-five percent. The money was minuscule. The first week we made fifty dollars, but I was happy because I did not have to work as a carpenter and get up at seven in the morning and go to the Bronx."

Frohlinde says he decided to sell chess sets from the studio. The profits began to rise. He advertised in magazines and newspapers. The monthly income increased until, he says, Rossolimo "came back from Paris and threw me out."

Frohlinde and his wife, Ruth, a German Jew who survived the Holocaust, opened a rival shop. He took many of the clients, as well as most of the inventory. Rossolimo, destitute and no longer playing much chess, tried to manage on his own. The two former partners did not speak, although their establishments were yards apart. Rossolimo worked out of a new shop on Thompson Street, during his last years. It would house the Chess Forum years later. The two men passed each other as if each were invisible. "You don't see people you don't like," Frohlinde says.

The grand master fell down a flight of stairs one July night in 1975 and died. His shop, run briefly by his widow, was closed a few months later.

"I didn't know he had died for a while," Frohlinde says. "At the time I did not have any particular feeling about it. He was old and drinking heavily."

The chess craze, ushered in by Bobby Fischer in the 1970s, hit the United States. Rossolimo, who made it into Fischer's book on the 100 greatest games he ever played, never capitalized on it, but Frohlinde did. He made money, big money, selling chess sets out of his shop.

"No one had chess sets for sale," he says. "When we saw that Fischer would probably become the world champion we bought lots of sets. When he did become champion, stores like Bloomingdale's had to send people down to see me to buy their sets for Christmas."

He opened a shop in Chicago and sold it at a tidy profit. But the craze faded with the demise of Fischer, who would go on to embrace bizarre politics and eccentricity. Age began to creep up on Frohlinde, just as it had with Rossolimo. He and Ruth, who was ill, began to think of retiring. And then another war, this time in the Middle East, cast a young Lebanese student and chess enthusiast named Imad Khachan on his doorstep.

Khachan was a graduate student at New York University. The fighting in Beirut had forced him to flee to Damascus and in 1988 to New York. He hoped to study literature, but money soon became a problem. He had few friends in the city. He went weeks

without speaking to anyone. The Lebanese war, its absurdity and
self-destructiveness, plagued him.

"The war in Lebanon became its own end," he says, seated in his
shop across the street. "It became like chess, moves that had no ultimate purpose other than to attack and defend. It was a free-for-
all. Allies turned on each other. Christians fought Christians.
Muslims fought Muslims. People are meaner to their own people.
Maybe this is human nature. You become more self-righteous with
your own family. You feel violence is more justified. You are the
big brother who will whip everyone into shape, even if you have to
kill them."

He went back to Beirut. The shells had blown apart so many
human bodies that he could smell the rot of decaying flesh hanging in the trees. He came back to New York. He left the English
department and transferred to Middle Eastern studies. His
scholarship did not cover his living expenses. He began to work
behind the counter at the Chess Shop. He was lonely and
knocked off balance by the brutality that was tearing apart his
country. He was unsure about what he wanted to do in life. He
was befriended by the German couple.. They asked him to manage the shop. He accepted and dropped out of school.

In 1990, four months into the job, Frohlinde proposed making
the young Lebanese the owner of the shop.

"I found it a little strange, but also flattering," he says.

Khachan said that the elderly German offered to sell the shop
for $500,000, a sum he could not raise or hope to get through
a loan. Instead, he would work the amount off until the shop
was his. He would work for five years and try to earn or bor-
row enough to pay the couple $100,000 a year. Khachan had
his hesitations. He was poor. It was a huge commitment. He sat
that evening and read the Koran, the Muslim holy book, for
guidance.

"I was reading about Moses," he says. "I was reading the story
about how he married his wife. In the Koranic version Moses

went to look for a well and saw two girls. He asked them the directions to the well. One of the women said she could show him the well. She told Moses to walk in front of her and she would direct him verbally from behind. But when Moses got to the well there was a huge stone. Moses, in the Koran, has superhuman strength and he lifted the stone. When Jethro saw the strength of Moses he asked him to run his farm for ten years. The woman became his wife. I read this story. I felt that in ten years I could take over the shop. The shop would be my bride. I got on the phone and called George. He drew up a typed agreement with his lawyer. I did not have a lawyer. I trusted George. I trusted his word."

But soon after the deal was struck Khachan said his salary began to be eaten up by the owners as payment for the shop. They argued about who owned the stock which Khachan said was worth about $300,000. He managed the shop, but the couple kept their hands tightly on the books and the bank accounts. He began to feel he was being had. He asked to see the books and he said they refused.

"Common sense should have told me this was not right," Khachan says, "that it would not work."

Khachan noticed that as his relationship with the couple soured, a strange thing happened between Frohlinde and his wife. They stopped their daily bickering and fighting.

"It was like the Lebanese civil war in that shop," Khachan says. "They fought over everything, with Ruth perched on her chair behind the counter like the queen. They read the papers all day and if anyone breathed or laughed too loudly God help them. But once they had a common enemy things changed. They put their own troubles on hold. They walked arm-in-arm. They laughed like young lovers. "

After months he got to look at the books. He says that the books showed that Frohlinde and his wife were each paid hefty salaries and had been reimbursed for many expenses.

Frohlinde, when I relay the story, dismisses Khachan's version of events. He says the young Lebanese never paid the money he had promised to buy the shop.

"He worked here," Frohlinde says of Khachan. "He learned the business. He found out all my suppliers and my customers and went across the street to open another store."

Khachan left the shop and borrowed money from friends and family. He opened the Chess Forum in 1995 in the same spot Rossolimo tried to run his studio. The war between Frohlinde and Rossolimo became the war between Frohlinde and Khachan. The anger and resentment, as it had before, severed all communication between the former partners. They passed on the street and did not acknowledge the other's presence.

"If I had to give him one book it would be *King Lear*," says Khachan of his former partner at the Chess Shop. "He is the man who divided his kingdom. This did not need to happen. The Chess Forum is George's legacy to himself. I never disobeyed George. He was like a father. But he created a feudal society. He thought he owned chess in New York. He thought no one could touch it but him. It was his kingdom. No one was entitled to challenge him."

The chess patrons were forced to choose between one shop or the other. There would be no toleration of those who crossed lines, especially by the crusty German who demanded absolute loyalty. Those who defected to the Chess Forum began to refer to Frohlinde as "the Nazi." Those in the Chess Shop began to call Khachan, a Muslim, "Yasir Arafat." It was, in the eyes of some of those who remained loyal to the Chess Shop, an act of betrayal for Jews to enter the Lebanese's chess shop.

Ruth, in failing health, hung on to the couple's shop, but in her last months could no longer work. Khachan said he mailed her a letter shortly before she died. It was his final effort to reach out to the couple.

"I told her I hoped she would get well," he says. "I told her in March or April, when the weather was better outside, I would come and sit with her and we would talk about the old days. She died not long after that."

But there would be no forgiveness or reconciliation. The hatred, nourished on years of rancor, stretching back half a decade with Rossolimo, was cherished by the two groups of chess players who sit for hours hunched over boards in the dingy shops. They need the rivalry to give drama to their lives. They may enjoy, as the couple did, having a common enemy. This comradeship creates a sense of belonging. It gives the two communities a sense of demarcation and importance. Reconciliation would mean facing lives without an epic battle. It would force them to focus on the harder task of living. The patrons of the two shops peer into each other's windows to feed the spiteful gossip. It is as if the old Russian grand master, who loved life a little too much, once made a record of Russian folk songs, drank in excess, drove a taxi and made it into Bobby Fischer's book on chess, is again alive. Rossolimo, it is whispered, although he may have been drinking the night he fell down the stairs, may also have been pushed. Intrigue heightens the drama.

Life is easier as a crusade. It gives the chess players dragons to slay. The hatred shuts out compassion. It focuses energy on destruction rather than affirmation. It consumes them.

The owners of the Chess Shop say they prohibit gambling. But their rivals, they contend, permit patrons to bet a dollar a game. Frohlinde's nephew and the current manager insist that "the park crowd," the hustlers who sit in Washington Square Park and play people for $5 a game, migrate to the Chess Forum late at night and continue to lure their prey.

"We try to keep our place pleasant with a family atmosphere," Nash says. "The other place is a lot more rambunctious."

Each owner tells me that packages destined for his shop, but delivered to the other by mistake, are never handed over, or sent back to suppliers. Although each owner also insists his shop has properly redirected wayward shipments.

Ernie Rosenberg tells me one afternoon as we stand amid the tables that he and his son were barred from entering the Chess Shop after they defected to the Chess Forum.

"I printed up leaflets and told the owners of the Chess Shop I would distribute them on the sidewalk during the Christmas season unless they lifted the ban on my son," he says. "Why did they ban my son? Because he was my son. My son did not really want to go there, but I got them to lift the ban. I used to go in and stand in the shop just to annoy them. They would try and throw me out."

Khachan adds that when he worked in the Chess Shop, "prices were inflated by thirty or forty percent" and "the place was crawling with cockroaches." He says the German couple reused tea bags for customers. With all the goings-on in the Chess Shop, he says, "it saves you from having to read Kafka."

"I can live with it," says Nash, seated in the Chess Shop when asked about the charges later that day, "although customers will go back and forth between the shops trying to lower the price on a set they want. We have had some bad price wars."

Khachan stands late in the evening in front of the plate glass window that displays his chess sets. He watches a young man in a black fatigue jacket and a black wool hat pulled down to his ears linger at his door. The man carries a folded chess board under his arm.

"He is a spy," Mr. Khachan tells me in a whisper. "He has been sent over to check the prices and count how many players are in my shop."

Nash, across the street, scoffs at the charge, calling Khachan paranoid.

"I have caught people Imad sent over to stand in front of our shop and tell customers his shop is better," he says. "He has been doing this for years. He doesn't let some customers into his shop because he says they are spies, but they are just players who like to play in both shops. It is all very weird."

GREED

You shall not covet your neighbor's house.

This is Karen Adey's dream. She will own a multimillion-dollar business. She will vacation on the Riviera. She will preside over a large and opulent home. She will be rich and powerful. Doors will open for her. People will clamor to be with her. They will relish the time in her presence, pay money for her services and thank her for making their lives fuller and happier. She will be in charge. She will be happy.

But until then she will have to be the tireless and devoted follower of self-help guru Anthony J. Robbins, whose seminars, books and cassette tapes and videos, which cost her thousands of dollars, will make her dream possible. She wants what Tony has, what he promises, what she believes he has become. She embraces his message of self-reliance, positive attitude, and studies his tips and techniques that will, once she masters them, make her the master. She is tired of following.

Adey says that the desire for wealth is not an end in itself. She hopes to attain wealth to do good. She does not see Robbins, or the techniques he teaches, as ones that are about coveting wealth and power. Yet the allure of fabulous wealth and power, and the respect and awe that comes with them, is the staple of his message, like that of television advertising and entertainment. It is fed to us in a multiplicity of images, in the stories about the famous and the rich, their yachts, their mansions, their jets, their vacations, their affairs and divorces. It is life on the other side. It appears, although this is part of the mirage, to be within our grasp if we pull the right levers and mutter the right incantations.

This desire is fueled by the two most destructive forces to happiness, envy and greed. It is fueled by the curse that has plagued us since the Enlightenment. This curse places humankind at the center of creation. It feeds us the impossible belief that there are no limits to what we can achieve. It tells us that we as individuals have an inestimable value and a God-given destiny. The goal of life becomes individual glory and greatness. The failure to achieve these aspirations, to be who we should be, seems to diminishes us. As we age, as life deals its blows of fortune and bad luck, as we face the harsh reality of human limitations, our own limitations, we become resentful. We hate ourselves for failing. We hate others who have less talent, less creativity, less integrity, yet seem to have risen above us. We war against others. We war against ourselves. We become isolated, living a lie, presenting to others, even those we love, an image of strength and optimism and success that clashes with our sea of insecurities and uncertainties. We silently tear ourselves apart. We are unhappy. We can fall into depression and loneliness, and feel trapped within the confines of a numbing social conformity. We seek refuge in antidepressants. This is the sickness of our age.

Robbins taps into this deep, burning insecurity. He knows how we view ourselves, our feelings of unworthiness. He knows too how we can be manipulated. He peddles hope, and hope is the market's most profitable commodity. The man or woman who has it all, who can make anything happen, is what we want to become. Robbins, to his followers, embodies this ideal. He promises to share it, to make us devine.

"I found myself comparing what I had to what other people had," says Adey, who first went to a motivational meeting run by

Robbins's franchise in 1994 in New Jersey. "It was that contrast—
it was keeping me from having the guts to do the things that
needed to be done. I was afraid to put myself out there."

I watch Robbins one morning in the theater in Madison
Square Garden. He warms up the crowd of several thousand who
had paid to attend his daylong seminar. He is imposing at six feet
seven inches with broad shoulders. He darts energetically back
and forth across the stage. His gestures are magnified on huge
video screens looming behind him. He wears a white shirt, a gold
tie and a black suit. He spits out aphorisms that excite the crowd,
most of whom were white, well dressed and middle-aged.

"How many of you had a goal, even achieved that goal, and
then the brain asked is that all there is?" he shouts into the microphone. "How many of you here would like to be outstanding?
Say 'I.'"

The crowd shouts "I."

He drops the names of celebrities such as Michael Jordan,
Tiger Woods and General Norman Schwarzkopf. He talks about
his $5.8 million castle in California, the resort he runs in Fiji, his
cars, his private jet and the huge multimillion-dollar contracts he
rejects because they are too low. And what he has, he insists, everyone can have.

"Everyone is crippled not by outside forces, but by themselves," Robbins says. "Today is about raising your standards. No
one follows a person whose standards are low. Our lives can
change in a minute. And today we have a lot of minutes together.
So you can change your life."

He tells his listeners they have a special purpose and are outstanding. He blasts music into the theater and has the crowd
stand on the chairs, pumping their fists into the air and singing
along with the Tina Turner song, "Simply the best, better than all
the rest." He high-fives those in the front rows. He throws off his
jacket. He calls out for the crowd to feel good, to begin to live a
life dominated by pleasure rather than pain. He says he can help

them train their nervous systems "to feel good all the time." He says that he can teach them how to influence people by interrupting patterns of conversation or mirroring behavior. He tells stories about how he cures phobias and stuttering. On the table in the lobby outside, he sells his books, videos and tapes along with vitamin supplements. His franchises earn him millions.

Several disgruntled former distributors, however, filed lawsuits against the Robbins operation in the 1990s, claiming either that they were not provided with promised backing and support or that exclusive territories were not, in fact, exclusive. Robbins described the allegations as "nonsense" and said that those who filed suit failed because they did not follow the successful formula they were trying to sell. "When somebody fails, the first person they blame is the franchisor," he said.[1] The Robbins operation, several years later, agreed to settle FTC charges of violating franchise disclosure rules and misrepresenting franchisees' potential sales and earnings. Although they acknowledged no wrongdoing, Robbins and his organization agreed to pay more than $220,000 to franchisees.[2]

But the public spat did not deter new recruits.

He speaks with a mixture of evangelical zeal—indeed he sounds like a circuit preacher—and uses personal testimonials. His signature stunt is to get followers to walk across hot coals— he calls it "fire walking"—to show that feet will not be burned "as long as you just believe!" The participants in Robbins's meetings break boards—karate style. They write their fears on the wood. His followers often return to event after event. They dole out increased sums to be inspired and empowered. Adey can repeat his aphorisms and inspirational sayings by heart. His followers blame themselves, not him, for their failures, believing they need a little more of the boost and the technique. The power to achieve is inside of them. The vast array of forces that shape and control them, from financial markets to banks, from industry flight to corporate greed, from government regulations and laws to fate itself, are irrelevant. They can mold the world.

His books are about the hidden potential within us. They have titles such as *Awaken the Giant Within: How to Take Immediate Control of Your Mental, Emotional, Physical and Financial Destiny.* Everyone can be Tony. And Tony is what everyone wants to become.

His message is a secular version of the television evangelist's gospel of greed and personal empowerment. Once you pay your tithe to these groups God will shower you with blessings. God will do your bidding. God will make you rich. The testimonials used by these multimillionaire television evangelists differ little from those used by Robbins. Robbins offers secular rather than divine tools to reach the same end. Each peddles a dangerous form of self-worship. They tap into the greed that runs like an electric current through America. They promise quick, easy shortcuts to get what we want, to become the idol we worship.

Life, Robbins says, should make us feel good. Nothing is supposed to hurt. All pain can be banished. He promises victory and success. We will be blissfully happy. We will become the center of the universe.

The desire for empowerment is enticing. It is difficult to accept our ordinariness. We look for escape routes to avoid the pitfalls of life, the hurts and rejections, the disappointments and frustrations, the inevitable tragedies. We want to be absolved of our responsibility for our neighbors and community. We want to replace it with the primacy of self. This desire fosters a dangerous kind of individualism. It allows us to rise on the backs of those we have been told should be manipulated for our gain. Those who suffer, those who fail, in this creed, do so because they are not good enough. The moral life becomes the life of achievement.

America's most pervasive idolatry is the idolatry of the self. This idolatry is fodder for the entertainment industry, plastic surgeons, fashion mavens and those who promise quick and easy ways to become rich and powerful. Americans spend an estimated $2.4 billion a year on the self-help industry, buying books such as Robbins's *Unlimited Power* and attending lectures and seminars. Robbins takes time to call on people to help those who are less fortunate, but his message is of charity, not justice. It is the wealthy doling out a few drops to the grateful masses, another form of self-adulation. And, implicit in his message, like those of the television preachers, is that the poor are poor because they are inadequate and undeserving.

"Tony does not teach people to covet," Adey insists. "Many people may come to his programs to learn to make more money. While they are there they begin to get the deeper message, the message that we all have something valuable to give back. People may feel they need a level of financial security before they begin thinking about giving their contribution to the world. This is the door Tony opens. People then make their own decision about whether they will go through that door or not."

Adey has a comfortable life. She has what most people on the planet could never hope to have: a pleasant home with her husband and two teenage children, in the leafy New Jersey suburb of Mendham. The bookshelves in her home office are filled with self-help titles like *The First Five Minutes, Making a Name for Yourself, The Truth About You, Highly Effective People* and *Frogs into Princes*. She is "a certified practitioner of neural linguistic programming," which she explains is a method of giving people techniques to get others to do what you want. The techniques include mirroring other people's behavior or making them associate pleasure with the product or service you hope to sell them. Pictures of her with Robbins are on the wall.

"Tony unlocks the code," she says. "It is like the Rosetta Stone. We know things about human interaction that can be quantified. He opened the curtain on that."

Adey carries in her pocketbook a laminated card with her goals for the yearly quarter. She runs her own company, Peak Strategies, which trains and coaches individuals in business development and marketing. It is a knockoff of Robbins's business. She ran another company, Advanced Visual Auditory and Kinesthetic, with a partner, but that venture was eventually abandoned. It too was an effort to sell techniques for personal empowerment. She struggles to find clients.

"The most important thing in my life is freedom," she says. "I want to go where I want, when I want, with whom I want, however I want, for as long as I want. Here I am in my fifties. I had never put this into words until the seminar. It made a lot of my life make sense."

She became a mother as a teenager. She divorced after a year and a half. She raised her first daughter for 13 years until marrying her present husband, Karl, who is 52. He is a quiet, guarded man who does not share his wife's enthusiasm for self-improvement or Robbins. He does not attend the seminars.

The couple lost their first house in Mendham to a fire in 1980. The event was deeply painful. She has never been able to extend Robbins's injunction to turn all personal tragedies into triumphs in the case of the fire.

"It is the only thing in my life I have never been able to see the good side of," she says.

The couple moved to Atlanta and later San Francisco. They took a second mortgage on their house in California to invest in a bakery. They lost the $50,000 they had put into the business. They went into foreclosure.

"We scrambled constantly with two little kids," she says. "We took in recycling for cash to get to work. We fought and we managed to make it. We borrowed from everyone we knew. We paid high interest. We paid penalties. We paid legal fees. It was a nightmare. The $50,000 is nothing compared to what we really lost. It was pushing $200,000 by the time we were done."

And then her husband lost his job. The family moved back to Mendham. They returned to New Jersey with as many financial troubles as when they left.

It was Robbins, Adey said, who helped motivate her to keep going. He taught her not to give up, to believe in her dreams and herself, all at a time when it seemed she could not face starting over. It was Robbins who gave her tools, she says, to get the world to begin to bend to her will. She believes she is on the cusp of mastering his techniques.

"The intent is to manipulate someone into doing something," she says, and then pauses before adding, "but let's face it, we are all manipulated all the time."

Her personal empowerment was strengthened through the seminars, especially when she walked on the hot coals or broke a board with her hands.

"I looked at the world and realized that I was not willing to let it ruin my life," she says. "I went through that board like it wasn't there. Everything shifted at that moment. I realized the only thing that stood between me and what I wanted was me."

All lives, at their deepest level, are failures. We fail to be the person we want to be; this is inevitable for we are human. We will fail to achieve all we want to achieve. We fail those we love in small and large ways. We are failed by them. We suffer betrayal and feel unappreciated. We are never as good as our expectations. We never overcome all our faults. We act in ways that are foolish, inconsistent, mean or thoughtless. This is part of our ordinariness, part of the failures inherent in human life. We live, however, in an unforgiving culture, one that tells us constantly that what we have, along with what we have achieved, is inadequate.

But only if we can accept our failures and our ordinariness, only if we can have the courage to face this wounding pain, can we find sustaining joy and happiness. The flight into the arms of self-help gurus like Robbins, who promise to banish insecurity and uncertainty, who promise to make us powerful and rich, has the opposite effect. We blame ourselves for failing to achieve these goals. We fear that underneath our facade we are the very people Robbins despises. We fear we are ordinary and fallible. We cannot forgive ourselves. We seek to cover up our weakness and our fear, we redouble our efforts to be extraordinary.

Fyodor Dostoyevsky in *Crime and Punishment* wrote of the danger behind this universal desire, this desire not to be ordinary but to be extraordinary. Raskolnikov, the main character in the novel, believed that humankind could be divided into two groups. The first was composed of ordinary people. These ordinary people were meek and submissive. They did little more than reproduce other human beings, grow old and die. And Robbins, like Raskolnikov, was dismissive of these lesser forms of human life.

The second group was extraordinary. These were, according to Raskolnikov, the Napoleons of the world, those who flaunted law and custom, those who shredded conventions and traditions to create a finer, more glorious future. Raskolnikov's theory was no different from Robbins's call for his followers to be outstanding. Robbins, like Raskolnikov, argues that, although we live in the world, we can free ourselves from the consequences of living with others, consequences that will not always be in our favor.

It is the tragedy of secular belief, indeed the tragedy of all man-made attempts at utopia, to place unbridled and total faith in the intellect. It is the worst form of self-devouring idolatry. As we realize that our attempts to achieve perfection are failing we become more afraid and more fanatic. Fear, in the end, drives us until we live lives dominated by fear.

The demented Raskolnikov murdered his landlady and began his slow, painful descent to self-realization, humility and finally atonement. He murdered because he was afraid he would not be extraordinary. He was afraid that one day he would vanish and never leave his mark. He was afraid that he would have to live constrained and penned in by social convention and middle-class morality. Raskolnikov, like many of us, believed that intellect was enough to order his life. He substituted intellect for faith. He made a god of his intellect and served this god. Like all false gods his intellect betrayed him.

The struggle Dostoyevsky chronicled in the novel is the struggle of those I watch in the theater. It is the struggle to accept who we are and our severe limitations. It is the struggle to accept that we are ordinary.

Happiness, Dostoyevsky wrote, cannot be achieved through the intellect. It cannot come from wealth or self-adulation. It can only come from self-sacrifice and the courage to accept suffering and failure as part of life. When we believe we can create a world that will ensure our personal happiness and success, a world that will make us extraordinary, a world without suffering, we fall into self-delusion. We lose touch with our own humanity and the humanity of those around us.

When Dante entered the "city of woes" in the *Inferno* he heard the cries of "those whose lives earned neither honor nor had fame," those rejected by Heaven and Hell, those who dedicated their lives solely to the pursuit of happiness. These were all the "nice" people, the ones who never made a fuss. They filled their lives with vain and empty pursuits, harmless no doubt, to amuse themselves. They never took a stand for anything, or risked anything. They went along. They never looked too hard at their lives, never felt the need, never wanted to look. They were propelled forward by the forces around them.

Courage is a primary virtue. It is needed to confront the inevitable disappointment that comes with living. We need to find the courage to become vulnerable. We need to find the courage to accept that we are not the sum of our achievements or wealth or power, but are the sum of all the tiny, unrecognized acts of love and kindness that get in the way of our careers, indeed may destroy our careers. Without courage we are not likely to practice any other virtues. Where courage is not, Samuel Johnson said, no other virtue can survive except by accident.

The most extraordinary, most exalted emotions in life appear in the mundane and the ordinary. It is compassion and affection that overcomes estrangement. It is in love that we find worth and happiness. But to love requires courage, not the physical courage of the battlefield, but the harder moral courage. It is difficult. To love deeply is to neglect "opportunities." It requires us to be ordinary. It may require us to give up our life.

"We all need to learn better how to love ourselves," the Reverend Coleman Brown wrote in his sermon "On Courage." "But courage is recognition that you can love your life too much; can love your life and, yes, your self too much—certainly in the wrong way."[3]

Those who love themselves above all others, who place themselves at the center of a self-created universe, are those who cannot love. They are left anguished, alone and bereft. Their fears multiply and overpower them. They flee, like Jonah, into the jaws of the monster they seek to escape. The willingness to sacrifice ourselves for others frees us from the insecurities and torment. It frees us to love. Josef Pieper in *The Four Cardinal Virtues* wrote:

> *To the modern science of psychology, we owe the insight that the lack of courage to accept injury and the incapability of self-sacrifice belong to the deepest sources of psychic illness. All neuroses seem to have as a common symptom an egocentric anxiety, a tense and self-centered concern for security, the inability to "let go"; in short, that kind of love for one's own life that leads straight to the loss of life. It is a very significant and by no means accidental fact that modern psychology frequently quotes the Scriptural words: "He who loves his life will lose it." Above and beyond their immediate religious significance they denote accurately the psychiatric-characterological diagnosis: that "the ego will become involved in ever greater danger the more carefully one tries to protect it."[4]*

I think of Moses as I watch Robbins, his voice booming over the amplified system, his constantly moving image towering above us on huge screens. Robbins offers the golden calf, the one Moses found the Israelites worshipping when he came down Mount Sinai with the tablets. The calf glitters before us in Madison Square Garden. It drives those around me faster and faster on the treadmill. We may be behind on mortgage and car payments, have credit card debt we can barely handle, struggle in a dead-end job we hate, neglect and be neglected by our friends and family; we might live so close to the margin we wonder some months how we're going to make it, but we will not give up the desperate dream. We need this dream, and the hope it can be fulfilled. We need it to cope with despair, the hard limitations of life, our smallness. To lose this hope means to acknowledge our weakness, our fear and our insignificance. It means being ordinary. We watch impassively as the wealthy and the elite, the huge corporations, rob us, ruin the environment, defraud consumers and taxpayers and create an exclusive American oligarchy that fuses wealth and political power. We watch passively because we believe we can enter the club. It is greed that inspires us. It is greed that keeps us silent. Our greed is devouring us.

Moses, after a long absence, came down the slopes of the mountain. He was clutching the tablets that contained the 10 Commandments, the rules that regulate ethical behavior and point the way to wholeness, the rules that give us life by cherishing all life. He, no speaker, no dandy, was enraged with the golden idol and Aaron, the idol's glib and popular priest. Moses, who would have been no match for Robbins, saw his people singing, and reveling around the calf. He dropped the tablets and they splintered into fragments. He ground the golden calf into dust and made the worshippers drink the bitter mixture. He turned on Aaron, the charlatan, the self-help guru, the one who fabricated the false god that told people what they wanted to hear.

I wonder what the crowd would do if Moses strode down the aisle with his long beard, knit brows and angry countenance. But Moses does not appear. No one stands up to debunk the imposter, the one who will fly home on his private jet to his mock castle by the sea with bundles of cash, the one who feeds them the lies they want to hear. Robbins stokes the fear they yearn to escape. He polishes the shanks of the golden calf. He calls us to kneel before it.

Adey will not give up. She is attempting to master the methods and the psychology that will finally persuade people to embrace her designs.

"You can plug into the way people are wired; I am not good at reading eye-access cues," she says, referring to techniques she uses to grasp people's thought processes. "It is something I am working on. When you master this, and I will master this, you can be another Tony."

She lives in the darkness of Robbins's shadow.

"I got to sit in his Bentley," says Adey, who has attended nearly a dozen seminars. "You could feel Tony's power."

Her husband, who has never been to an event run by Robbins, grew up on a farm in Pennsylvania, where "people don't talk much about themselves," he tells me. He works as a computer technician for a company in Newark. He plans to retire to a farm. His wife does not greet the idea with enthusiasm.

"You can't take care of animals when you are in the Riviera," she says.

"I won't be going to the Riviera," he answers.

———◆———

LOVE

My children will soon be young adults. They are breaking, as they must in our culture, the oppressive bond of the parent, to become distinct individuals. I walk by their rooms at night and sometimes feel a catch in my throat. I picture the day when the house will be empty. The small agonies and heartbreaks, the triumphs at school or on a soccer field, the long discussions, the intimate life of our family will change, kept alive by common memories, visits and sporadic conversations. But this too will become less vivid. I dread the time the children leave. This is what it means to be a parent. It hurts. All love hurts.

My life as a war correspondent is over. The names of the conflicts I covered are only vaguely familiar to my students. The civil wars in El Salvador or Algeria or the Sudan belong to another time, another age of passion and blood. I carry within me these shards and fragments of memories, some of which I would like to forget. These pieces of a life are finally incomprehensible. We are not the sum of events, although those on the outside sometimes use events to define us. We are not our titles or positions or accomplishments. We are distinct from these. We puzzle over ourselves as time, with its ruthless and swift gait, sweeps our lives into the past. The lives that went before mine, the lives that will come after mine, seem sometimes to merge, bound together by common rituals, the physical and spiritual wanderings that come with human existence and the strangeness of it all.

I am writing this on a winter night in a small house on a hilltop in Maine. The wind is rattling the panes of frosted glass. The cold air seeps in through the cracks of the house despite a fire and the cloth pads under the door jams and along the windows. The snow blankets the slope that runs down toward the silhouettes of barren, leafless trees. It has been almost a century since my grandparents gathered on summer afternoons in coats and ties or white dresses not far from my door. The forest has reclaimed the meadow where they sat on blankets, eating lunch from a basket. The trees, laden with ice and snow, whisper their presence.

I have sepia photographs that show bright faces of these young men and women, whom I would only know in old age, ready to embark on life. They radiate hope and promise. They trust in the future. I know the heartaches and struggles before them, heartaches they could not have imagined when the pictures were taken. Most of them will spend their lives working in shoe shops and paper and lumber mills. They will know poverty, be touched and maimed by war and disease, raise children and bury some of them, have happy and unhappy marriages and late in life take a small child, who decades later would write about them, to the creeks, lakes and woods where they spent the quieter days of youth. There is a stone wall surrounding a cemetery at the end of the dirt road running from the house. My father is buried there. I am the father now. This too will change.

It does not matter how astutely we move the pieces on the chessboard. The game of life and death is a game we lose. Perhaps there will be a final reckoning at the end, a looking back on it all, but more likely our last moments will be devoted to summoning the momentous energy to gulp down one more breath amid blinking lights and the hum of the hospital monitors. I have seen enough of death to know its ugly and tawdry face. It is coming. It comes for all of us. Time is short. Life is brief.

Love means living for others. Many parents know this sacrifice, not the temporary sacrifice made to assist another, but the daily sacrifice to create life at the expense of our pleasure, career and dreams. There is drudgery and difficulty in this self-denial. It is not easy. But by giving up parts of ourselves for others, by accepting that we must be willing to lose life to create and preserve life, we honor the core of the commandments. The commandments hold out to us the possibility of love. Those who have this love are able to receive and give love to others. Those who do not know this love live in Dostoyevsky's hell. The worst torment in life, the torment known to H. R. Vargas, Patrick and Tyrone, is the torment of being exiled to a life without love. Love is the mysterious life force that comes closest to putting us in touch with the power and majesty of God. It is the spark of divinity we carry within us. It is what we pass on to others. It is life. The more we reach out to sustain life, as individuals, as communities and as a nation, the more we affirm that which we know we must affirm. The more we fold in on ourselves, worshipping not the sanctity of life but the forces that empower and enrich us at the expense of others, the more we kneel before the idols that will eventually slay us. All the explosions and attacks in Iraq, symbols of our might and power, are steadily corrupting the soul of our nation, deforming and maiming the young men and women who will return home to us broken, disillusioned and haunted by the murder and killing we made them commit. The commandments will speak to them in ways they never imagined, just as they speak bitterly to the Iraqis whose lives we have irrevocably ruined.

We all stray. We all violate some commandments and do not adequately honor others. We are human. But the commandments bind us together. They work to keep us from revering the *false covenants* that destroy us. These false covenants have a powerful appeal. They offer a sense of security and empowerment. They tempt us to be God. They tell us the things we want to hear and believe. They appear to make us the center of the universe. They make us feel we belong. But these false covenants, covenants built around exclusive communities of race, gender, class, religion and nation, inevitably carry within them the denigration of others who we exclude. These false covenants divide us. The covenant offered by the commandments, the covenant of life, is the covenant of love. It is a covenant that recognizes that all life is sacred and love is the force that makes life together possible.

It is the unmentioned fear of death and obliteration, the one that rattles with the wind through the heavy branches of the trees outside, which frightens us most, even as we do not name this fear. It is death we are fleeing. The smallness of our lives, the transitory nature of existence, the inevitable road to old age, are what idols tell us we can avoid. They lie, promising us routes out of the forest. The false covenants, which require us to break the commandments, tell us that we need not endure the pain and suffering of human existence. We follow the idol and barter away our freedom. We place our identity and our hopes in the hands of the idol. We believe we need the idol to define ourselves, to determine our worth. We invest in the idol. We sell ourselves into bondage.

The consumer goods we amass, the status we seek in titles and positions, the ruthlessness we employ to advance our careers, the ambitions and even noble causes we champion, the money we covet and the houses we build and the cars we drive become our pathetic statements of being. The more we strive the more intolerant we become. And those of us who see the truth of the commandments have a hard time applying them. It is one thing to understand but another to act. It is easy to be overwhelmed by the noise and images and self-gratification. It is easy to play the game. Impulses and emotions, not thoughts but mass feelings, propel us forward. These impulses, carefully manipulated, intox-

icate us with patriotic fervor and a lust for war. They lead us to
support candidates who appeal to us emotionally or to buy a certain product or brand. Politicians, advertisers, social scientists,
television evangelists, the news media and the entertainment industry have learned what makes us respond. It works. None of us
are immune. But when we act in their interests we are rarely act-
ing in our own. The commandments serve as a check on the del-
uge. They point us away from the city of man toward the city of
God. They do not call us to practice total self-abnegation, empowering others, as I did at first in Roxbury, to abuse us. They
call us rather toward mutual respect and mutual self-sacrifice.
The commandments were not written so they could be practiced
by some and not by others. They call on us all to curb our worst
instincts so we can live together, to refrain from committing the
acts of evil that spread hatred and death, rather than love, into
the world around us.

The commandments are guideposts. They bring us back, even
when we stray, as we all do, to the right path. They are our protection against the siren calls of glory, wealth and power that will
ultimately dash us against the rocks. We often want to take the
easy route. We do not want to sacrifice. We pay money to self-
help gurus or join the Latin Kings to find power and adulation.
We become professional killers in the army and are decorated
and lauded by the state for acts that violate the commandments.
But we pay with our souls. No one in this book violated the commandments without tremendous anguish and no one suffered violations without great pain. They did not have, in many cases,
control over the commandments that dominated their lives. The
commandments chose them. But it is never too late to turn back.
Atonement permits a new way of being. It calls us to life.

The strange fragments of our lives can only be comprehended
when we accept our insecurities and uncertainties, when we accept that we will never know what life is about or what it is supposed to mean, when we accept that we are ordinary. We must do

the best we can, not for ourselves, the commandments teach us, but for those around us. It is in this darkness, this mystery of existence, that we learn to trust. Trust is the compound that unites us. Life comes with giving life to others. We are the product of what came before. The children asleep in the rooms above me are what will follow. The quality of our life, of all life, is determined by what we give and what we sacrifice. We live, the commandments tell us, not by exalting our life but by being willing to lose it.

NOTES

PROLOGUE

1. Krzysztof Kieslowski interview, Denver International Film Festival, quoted in M. S. Mason, "Usually-fluffy TV digs a bit deeper," *Christian Science Monitor,* May 12, 2000. http://csmonitor.com/cgibin/durableRedirect.pl?/durable/2005/05/12/text/p18s1.html

2. Kieslowski, quoted in Roger Ebert, "The Decalogue," *Chicago Sun-Times,* April 2, 2000. http://www.suntimes.com/ebert/greatmovies/decalogue.html

3. Ludwig Wittgenstein, *Philosophical Grammar,* ed. R. Rhees, trans. Anthony Kenny (Oxford: Oxford University Press, 1974), 370; cited by Paul Holmer, *The Grammar of Faith* (San Francisco: Harper & Row, 1978), 185.

DECALOGUE I: MYSTERY

1. Fyodor Dostoyevsky, *The Brothers Karamazov,* trans. Richard Pevear and Larissa Volokhonsky (New York: Alfred A. Knopf, 1992), 313–14.

2. Ibid., 322.

3. Mark Twain, *The Works of Mark Twain: Early Tales & Sketches, Volume 1, 1851–1864,* ed. Edgar Marquess Branch and Robert H. Hirst (Berkeley: University of California Press, 1979), 368. The quotation reads ". . . with the serene confidence which a Christian feels in four aces."

DECALOGUE II: IDOLS

1. Exodus 3:14 Revised Standard Version.

2. Dietrich Bonhoeffer, *Letters and Papers from Prison,* enlarged edition, ed. Eberhard Bethge (New York: Touchstone, 1971), 8.

3. William Stringfellow, *A Private and Public Faith* (Grand Rapids, MI: William B. Eerdmans Publishing Company, 1962), 48.

DECALOGUE III: LYING

1. Elias Canetti, *Crowds and Power,* trans. Carol Stewart (New York: Farrar, Straus and Giroux, 1984), 210.
2. W. H. Auden, "September 1, 1939," in *Selected Poems,* ed. Edward Mendelson (London: Faber & Faber, 1979), 87.

DECALOGUE IV: THE SABBATH

1. Abraham Heschel, *The Insecurity of Freedom: Essays on Human Existence* (New York: Schocken, 1972), 5.

DECALOGUE V: THE FAMILY

1. William Shakespeare, *Love's Labor's Lost,* in *The Riverside Shakespeare,* 2nd edition, ed. G. Blakemore Evans and J. J. M. Tobin (Boston: Houghton Mifflin, 1997), 5.2.752.
2. Ibid., 5.2.850–56.
3. Ibid., 5.2.930–31.
4. Lionel Salter, booklet translation for Giacomo Puccini, *Tosca,* Philadelphia Orchestra, Riccardo Muti, Philips DDD 434 595–2, 146.
5. Ibid., 156.
6. André Malraux, *Anti-Memoirs,* trans. Terence Kilmartin (New York: Holt, Rinehart and Winston, 1968), 102.
7. Chris Hedges, *Granta 84,* "Over There: How America Sees the World," January 1, 2004.

DECALOGUE VI: MURDER

1. T. S. Eliot, "Gerontion," *Selected Poems* (New York: Harcourt, Brace & World, 1964), 32.
2. William P. Mahedy, *Out of the Night: The Spiritual Journey of Vietnam Vets* (New York: Ballantine Books, 1986), 7.
3. Ibid., 7.
4. Ibid., 115.

DECALOGUE VII: ADULTERY

1. Gardner C. Taylor, "Making a Great Promise Reasonable," *The Scarlet Thread* (Elgin, IL: Progressive Baptist Publishing House, 1981), 50f.
2. Sebastian Haffner, *Defying Hitler,* trans. Oliver Pretzel (New York: Farrar, Straus and Giroux, 2002), 288.
3. Hannah Arendt, *The Origins of Totalitarianism* (New York: Harcourt Brace, 1979), 478.

DECALOGUE VIII: THEFT

1. U.S. Senate Committee on Governmental Affairs, *The Role of the Board of Directors in Enron's Collapse,* 107th Cong., 2d sess., 2002, Rept. 107–70, 58.

2. David Callahan, *The Cheating Culture : Why More Americans Are Doing Wrong to Get Ahead* (New York: Harcourt, 2004), 67.

3. Russell Mokhiber and Robert Weissman, "Blue Cross, Blue Shield, Blue Criminal," *Corporate Predators: The Hunt for Mega-Profits and the Attack on Democracy* (Monroe, Maine: Common Courage Press, 1999), 19.

4. Russell Mokhiber, "Soft on Crime," *Multinational Monitor,* May 1, 1995.

5. Callahan, 67.

6. Ibid., 165.

7. Amy Goodman with David Goodman, *The Exception to the Rulers: Exposing Oily Politicians, War Profiteers, and the Media That Love Them* (New York: Hyperion, 2004), 65–66.

8. Robert Scheer, "Dick Cheney's Slimy Business Trail," *Salon.com,* July 17, 2002. http//www.salon.com/news/col/scheer/2002/07/17/cheney/

9. Goodman, 66–67.

10. Ibid., 68.

11. Ruth Rosen, "As Ordered, It's About Oil," *San Francisco Chronicle,* August 8, 2003, final edition.

12. Hannah Arendt, "Truth and Politics" in *The Portable Hannah Arendt,* ed. Peter Baehr (New York: Penguin, 2000), 568.

13. John S. Carroll, "The Wolf in Reporter's Clothing: The Rise of Pseudo-Journalism in America," 2004 Ruhl Lecture on Ethics delivered at the School of Journalism and Communication, University of Oregon, Eugene, May 6, 2004. http://www.latimes.com/news/opinion/commentary/la-050604ruhllecture_lat.story

14. Joseph Conrad, *Heart of Darkness,* in *Three Short Novels* (New York: Bantam Books, 1960), 31.

15. Sissela Bok, *Lying: Moral Choice in Public and Private Life* (New York: Vintage Books, 1989), 32–46.

16. Immanual Kant, *The Doctrine of Virtue: Part II of the Metaphysic of Morals,* trans. Mary J. Gregor (New York: Harper & Row, 1964), 93.

DECALOGUE X: GREED

1. Andrew LePage, "Distributors Sue Robbins, Ask for Millions in Damages," *San Diego Business Journal,* September 16, 1991. See also Michael Granberry, "Walking on Hot Coals: Lawsuits Pile Up for Motivational Guru Robbins," *Los Angeles Times,* September 9, 1991.

2. Federal Trade Commission, Office of Public Affairs, "Anthony Robbins Agrees to Pay More than $200,000 in Consumer Redress to Settle Alleged Franchise Rule Violations," May 16, 1995. http://www.ftc.gov/opa/1995/05/robbins.htm

3. Coleman Brown, "On Courage," in *Our Hearts Are Restless Till They Find Their Rest in Thee: Selected Sermons to the Colgate University Church, 1974–1989* (Sherburne, NY: Kenyon Press, 2003), 64.

4. Josef Pieper, *The Four Cardinal Virtues* (Notre Dame, IN: University of Notre Dame Press, [1954 etc.] 1966): 134, cited by Coleman Brown, "On Courage. 64–65.

BIBLIOGRAPHY

———

Aeschylus. *The Oresteia.* Translated by Robert Fagles. New York: Penguin, 1979.

Alter, Robert. *The Art of Biblical Narrative.* New York: Basic Books, 1981.

Arendt, Hannah. *Love and Saint Augustine.* Chicago: University of Chicago Press, 1996.

———. *On Revolution.* New York: Penguin, 1985.

———. *On Violence.* New York: Harcourt Brace Jovanovich, 1970.

———. *The Origins of Totalitarianism.* New York: Harcourt Brace, 1979.

———. *Responsibility and Judgment.* New York: Schocken, 2003.

———. "Truth and Politics." In *The Portable Hannah Arendt.* Edited by Peter Baehr. New York: Penguin, 2000.

Armstrong, Karen. *The Battle for God.* New York: Knopf, 2000.

Auden, W. H. *Collected Shorter Poems, 1927–1957.* New York: Vintage, 1975.

———. *Selected Poems.* Edited by Edward Mendelson. London: Faber & Faber, 1979.

Barth, Karl. *The Epistle to the Romans.* Translated by Edwyn Hoskyns. London: Oxford University Press, 1977.

Bartov, Moer. *Mirrors of Destruction: War, Genocide and Modern Identity.* New York: Oxford University Press, 2000.

——. *Murder in Our Midst: The Holocaust, Industrial Killing, and Representation.* New York: Oxford University Press, 1996.

Bate, W. Jackson. *Samuel Johnson.* New York: Harcourt Brace Jovanovich, 1977.

Berlin, Isaiah. *The Proper Study of Mankind.* New York: Farrar, Straus and Giroux, 1998.

Bettelheim, Bruno. *The Uses of Enchantment.* New York: Vintage, 1989.

Bok, Sissela. *Lying: Moral Choice in Public and Private Life.* New York: Vintage, 1989.

——. *Secrets: On the Ethics of Concealment and Revelation.* New York: Vintage, 1989.

Bonhoeffer, Dietrich. *The Cost of Discipleship.* Translated by R. H. Fuller. New York: Touchstone, 1995.

——. *Ethics.* Translated by Neville Horton Smith. New York: Touchstone, 1995.

——. *Letters and Papers from Prison.* Enlarged Edition. Edited by Eberhard Bethge. New York: Touchstone, 1971.

Borg, Marcus J. *Meeting Jesus Again for the First Time: The Historical Jesus & the Heart of Contemporary Faith.* San Francisco: HarperSan Francisco, 1994.

Bornkamm, Günther. *Jesus of Nazareth.* Translated by Irene and Fraser McLuskey. New York: Harper & Row, 1975.

Bourne, Randolph. *The Radical Will: Selected Writings, 1911–1918.* Berkeley: University of California Press, 1982.

Brinton, Crane. *The Shaping of Modern Thought.* Englewood Cliffs, NJ: Prentice-Hall, 1963.

Brodsky, Joseph. *Less Than One.* London: Penguin, 1987.

Brown, Coleman. *Our Hearts Are Restless Till They Find Their Rest in Thee: Selected Sermons to the Colgate University Church, 1974–1989.* Sherburne, NY: Kenyon Press, 2003.

Brown, Peter. *Augustine of Hippo*. Berkeley: University of California Press, 2000.

Brown, Robert McAfee, ed. *The Essential Reinhold Niebuhr*. New Haven: Yale University Press, 1986.

Brunschwig, Jacque and Geoffrey E. R. Lloyd, eds. *Greek Thought: A Guide to Classical Knowledge*. Cambridge, MA: Harvard University Press, 2000.

Buber, Martin. *I and Thou*. Translated by Walter Kaufman. New York: Charles Scribner's Sons, 1970.

———. *Moses: The Revolution and the Conenant*. New York: Harper Torchbooks, 1958.

Bultman, Rudolf. *Theology of the New Testament*. Translated by Kendrick Grobel. New York: Charles Scribner's Sons, 1955.

Callahan, David. *The Cheating Culture : Why More Americans Are Doing Wrong to Get Ahead*. New York: Harcourt, 2004.

Camus, Albert. *Exile and the Kingdom*. Translated by Justin O'Brien. New York: Penguin, 1962.

———. *The First Man*. Translated by David Hapgood. New York: Knopf, 1995.

———. *The Myth of Sisyphus*. Translated by Justin O'Brien. New York: Penguin, 1955.

———. *The Outsider*. Translated by Joseph Laredo. New York: Penguin, 1983.

———. *The Plague*. Translated by Stuart Gilbert. New York: Vintage International, 1991.

———. *The Rebel*. Translated by Anthony Boxer. New York: Penguin, 1986.

Canetti, Elias. *Crowds and Power*. New York: Farrar, Straus and Giroux, 1984.

Cicero. *On the Good Life*. Translated by Michael Grant. New York: Penguin, 1971.

Conrad, Joseph. *Heart of Darkness*. In *Three Short Novels*. New York: Bantam Books, 1960.

————. *Lord Jim*. Evanston, IL: Harper & Row, 1963.

Crossman, Richard, ed. *The God That Failed*. Chicago: Regnery Gateway, 1983.

Dante. *The Inferno of Dante*. Translated by Robert Pinsky. New York: Noonday Press, 1994.

Dostoyevsky, Fyodor. *The Brothers Karamazov*. Translated by Richard Pevear and Larissa Volokhonsky. New York: Alfred A. Knopf, 1992.

————. *Crime & Punishment*. Translated by Constance Garnett. New York: Modern Library, 1978.

Eco, Umberto. *Five Moral Pieces*. Translated by Alastair McEwen. New York: Harvest Books, 2001.

Eksteins, Modris. *Rites of Spring*. New York: Mariner, 2000.

Eliot, T. S. *Selected Poems*. New York: Harcourt, Brace & World, 1964.

Ellul, Jacques. *The Technological Society*. Translated by John Wilkinson. New York: Vintage, 1964.

Elshtain, Jean Bethke. *Jane Addams and the Dream of American Democracy*. New York: Basic Books, 2001.

Foucault, Michel. *Discipline and Punish*. Translated by Alan Sheridan. New York: Vintage, 1979.

Fox, Richard. *Reinhold Niebuhr: A Biography*. New York: Pantheon, 1985.

Frankl, Viktor. *Man's Search for Meaning*. New York: Touchstone, 1984.

French, Peter. *The Virtues of Vengeance*. Lawrence, KS: University Press of Kansas, 2001.

Freud, Sigmund. *Civilization and Its Discontents*. Translated by James Strachey. New York: W. W. Norton, 1989.

————. *Group Psychology and the Analysis of the Ego*. Translated by James Strachey. New York: W. W. Norton, 1989.

Fromm, Erich. *Escape from Freedom*. New York: Henry Holt, 1994.

————. *Psychoanalysis and Religion*. New York: Bantam Books, 1972.

Frye, Northrop. *The Great Code: The Bible and Literature.* New York: Harcourt Brace Jovanovich, 1982.

Fukuyama, Francis. *The End of History and the Last Man.* New York: Penguin, 1992.

Fussell, Paul. *The Great War and Modern Memory.* New York: Oxford University Press, 1977.

Gerson, Lloyd, ed. *The Cambridge Companion to Plotinus.* Cambridge, UK: Cambridge University Press, 1999.

Gide, André. *The Counterfeiters.* Translated by Dorothy Bussy. New York: Penguin, 1982.

———. *If I Die . . .* Translated by Dorothy Bussy. New York: Penguin, 1982.

Goldstone, Jack. *Revolution and Rebellion in the Early Modern World.* Berkeley: University of California Press, 1991.

Goodman, Amy, with David Goodman. *The Exception to the Rulers: Exposing Oily Politicians, War Profiteers, and the Media That Love Them.* New York: Hyperion, 2004.

Govier, Trudy. *Forgiveness and Revenge.* London: Routledge, 2002.

Graves, Robert. *The Greek Myths: Volume One.* New York: Penguin, 1960.

———. *The Greek Myths: Volume Two.* New York: Penguin, 1960.

Gray, J. Glenn. *The Warriors: Reflections on Men in Battle.* Lincoln, NE: University of Nebraska Press, 1998.

Grossman, Dave. *On Killing: The Psychological Cost of Learning to Kill in War and Society.* Boston: Little, Brown, 1995.

Grossman, Vasily. *Life and Fate.* Translated by Robert Chandler. New York: Harper & Row, 1987.

Haffner, Sebastian. *Defying Hitler.* Translated by Oliver Pretzel. New York: Farrar, Straus and Giroux, 2002.

Hartshorne, M. Holmes. *Speaking.* Hamilton, NY: Colgate University, 1998.

Hedges, Chris. *War Is a Force That Gives Us Meaning.* New York: Anchor Books, 2002.

Herman, Judith. *Trauma and Recovery*. New York: Basic Books, 1997.

Heschel, Abraham. *Between God and Man: An Interpretation of Judaism*. New York: Free Press, 1965.

——. *The Insecurity of Freedom: Essays on Human Existence*. New York: Schocken, 1972.

——. *The Quest for God*. New York: Charles Scribner's Sons, 1954.

——. *The Sabbath*. New York: Farrar, Straus and Giroux, 2001.

Horney, Karen. *Our Inner Conflicts*. New York: W. W. Norton, 1966.

Hynes, Samuel. *The Soldiers' Tale: Bearing Witness to Modern War*. New York: Penguin, 1997.

Ignatieff, Michael. *Isaiah Berlin: A Life*. New York: Metropolitan, 1998.

——. *The Warrior's Honor*. New York: Henry Holt, 1997.

Jacobi, Jolande. *The Psychology of C. G. Jung*. Translated by Ralph Manheim. New Haven: Yale University Press, 1973.

James, William. *The Varieties of Religious Experience*. New York: Touchstone, 1997.

Jung, Carl Gustav. ed. *Man and His Symbols*. New York: Dell, 1977.

——. *Psychology and Religion*. New Haven: Yale University Press, 1938.

Kant, Immanuel. *The Doctrine of Virtue: Part II of the Metaphysic of Morals*. Translated by Mary J. Gregor. New York: Harper & Row, 1964.

Kedourie, Elie. *Nationalism*. Oxford: Blackwell, 1996.

Ketwig, John. *. . . and a hard rain fell*. Naperville, IL: Sourcebooks, 2002.

Kierkegaard, Søren. *Fear and Trembling and the Sickness Unto Death*. Translated by Walter Lowrie. Princeton: Princeton University Press, 1974.

——. *Purity of Heart Is to Will One Thing*. Translated by Douglas Steere. New York: Harper Torchbooks, 1956.

———. *Works of Love.* Translated by Howard and Edna Hong. New York: Harper Torchbooks, 1964.

Kieslowski, Krzysztof. *The Decalogue.* 584 mins. Facets Video release of a Telewizja Polska production, 1988. DVD.

Knox, Bernard. *Essays Ancient and Modern.* Baltimore: Johns Hopkins University Press, 1989.

Le Bon, Gustave. *The Crowd: A Study of the Popular Mind.* Mineola, NY: Dover, 2002.

LeShan, Lawrence. *The Psychology of War: Comprehending Its Mystique and Its Madness.* New York: Helios, 2002.

Levi, Primo. *If This Is a Man / The Truce.* Translated by Stuart Woolf. New York: Vintage, 1996.

———. *Survival in Auschwitz.* Translated by Stuart Woolf. New York: Collier, 1961.

Lippmann, Walter. *Public Opinion.* New York: Free Press, 1997.

Mahedy, William P. *Out of the Night: The Spiritual Journey of Vietnam Vets.* New York: Ballantine Books, 1986.

Malraux, André. *Anti-Memoirs.* Translated by Terence Kilmartin. New York: Holt, Rinehart and Winston, 1968.

———. *Man's Hope.* Translated by Stuart Gilbert and Alastair Macdonald. New York: Grove, 1979.

Mandelstam, Nadezhda. *Hope Against Hope.* Translated by Max Hayward. London: Collins and Harvill, 1971.

Milosz, Czeslaw. *The Captive Mind.* Translated by Jane Zielonko. New York: Vintage, 1981.

Milton, John. *Paradise Lost.* Norton Critical Edition. Second Edition. Edited by Scott Elledge. New York: W. W. Norton, 1975.

Minow, Martha. *Between Vengeance and Forgiveness.* Boston: Beacon, 1998.

Mokhiber, Russell and Robert Weissman. "Blue Cross, Blue Shield, Blue Criminal." In *Corporate Predators: The Hunt for Mega-Profits and the Attack on Democracy.* Monroe, Maine: Common Courage Press, 1999.

Murphy, Jeffrie and Jean Hampton. *Forgiveness and Mercy*. Cambridge, UK: Cambridge University Press, 1998.

Neiman, Susan. *Evil in Modern Thought*. Princeton: Princeton University Press, 2002.

Niebuhr, Reinhold. *Beyond Tragedy: Essays on the Christian Interpretation of History*. New York: Charles Scribner's Sons, 1965.

———. *The Children of Light and the Children of Darkness*. New York: Charles Scribner's Sons, 1972.

———. *Faith and History: A Comparison of Christian and Modern Views of History*. New York: Charles Scribner's Sons, 1949.

———. *An Interpretation of Christian Ethics*. New York: Seabury Press, 1979.

———. *The Irony of American History*. New York: Charles Scribner's Sons, 1952.

———. *Justice and Mercy*. New York: Harper & Row, 1974.

———. *Leaves from the Notebook of a Tamed Cynic*. New York: Da Capo Press, 1976.

———. *Love and Justice: Selections from the Shorter Writings of Reinhold Niebuhr*. Louisville, KY: Westminster/John Knox Press, 1957.

———. *Moral Man and Immoral Society*. Eugene, OR: Wipf and Stock, 2001.

———. *The Nature and Destiny of Man, Volume One: Human Nature*. New York: Charles Scribner's Sons, 1964.

———. *The Nature and Destiny of Man, Volume Two: Human Destiny*. New York: Charles Scribner's Sons, 1964.

Orwell, Sonia, and Ian Angus, eds. *The Collected Essays, Journalism and Letters of George Orwell (Vols. 1–4)*. New York: Harcourt Brace Jovanovich, 1968.

Paz, Octavio. *The Labyrinth of Solitude*. New York: Grove Weidenfeld, 1985.

Percy, Walter. *The Thanatos Syndrome*. New York: Farrar, Straus and Giroux, 1987.

Plato. *Five Great Dialogues*. Translated by B. Jowett. Roslyn, NY: Walter J. Black, Inc., 1942.

Plotinus. *The Enneads*. Translated by Stephen MacKenna. Burdett, NY: Larson, 1992.

Popper, Karl. *The Open Society and Its Enemies: Plato*. Princeton: Princeton University Press, 1971.

———. *The Open Society and Its Enemies: Hegel and Marx*. Princeton: Princeton University Press, 1971.

———. *The Poverty of Historicism*. London: Routledge, 1991.

Postman, Neil. *Amusing Ourselves to Death*. New York: Penguin, 1985.

———. *The Disappearance of Childhood*. New York: Vintage, 1994.

Puccini, Giacomo. *Tosca*. Philadelphia Orchestra. Riccardo Muti. Philips DDD 434 595–2.

Roskill, Mark, ed. *The Letters of Vincent van Gogh*. New York: Touchstone, 1997.

St. Augustine. *City of God*. Translated by Henry Bettenson. London: Penguin Classics, 2003.

———. *Confessions*. Translated by R. S. Pine-Coffin. New York: Penguin, 1982.

St. Matthew, St. Mark, St. Luke, St. John. *The Illustrated Gospels*. New York: Crown, 1985.

Shakespeare, William. *The Riverside Shakespeare*, 2nd ed. Edited by G. Blakemore Evans and J. J. Tobin. Boston: Houghton Mifflin, 1997.

Shay, Jonathan. *Achilles in Vietnam*. New York: Touchstone, 1995.

Siemon-Netto, Uwe. *The Acquittal of God: A Theology for Vietnam Veterans*. New York: Pilgrim, 1990.

Silkin, Jon, ed. *The Penguin Book of First World War Poetry*. London: Penguin, 1996.

Silverman, Ray, and Star Silverman. *Rise Above It: Spiritual Development Through the Ten Commandments*. Philadelphia: Touchstone Seminars, 2000.

Sontag, Susan. *Illness as Metaphor and AIDS as a Metaphor*. New York: Anchor, 1990.

———. *Styles of Radical Will*. New York: Anchor, 1991.

———. *Under the Sign of Saturn.* New York: Anchor, 1991.

Sophocles. *Oedipus Tyrannus.* Translated by Peter Meineck and Paul Woodruff. Indianapolis: Hackett, 2000.

———. *The Three Theban Plays.* Translated by Robert Fagels. New York: Penguin, 1984.

Stendahl, Krister. *Meanings: The Bible as Document and as Guide.* Philadelphia: Fortress, 1984.

Stern, Gerald. *What I Can't Bear Losing.* New York: W. W. Norton, 2004.

Stringfellow, William. *Dissenter in a Great Society: A Christian View of America in Crisis.* New York: Holt, Rinehart and Winston, 1966.

———. *An Ethic for Christians and Other Aliens in a Strange Land.* Waco, TX: Word Books, 1973.

———. *My People Is the Enemy.* New York: Holt, Rinehart and Winston, 1964.

———. *A Private and Public Faith.* Grand Rapids, MI: William B. Eerdmans Publishing Company, 1962.

Taylor, Gardner C. "Making a Great Promise Reasonable." In *The Scarlet Thread.* Elgin, IL: Progressive Baptist Publishing House, 1981.

Thomas, Keith. *Religion and the Decline of Magic.* New York: Charles Scribner's Sons, 1971.

Tillich, Paul. *Biblical Religion and the Search for Ultimate Reality.* Chicago: University of Chicago Press, 1972.

———. *The Eternal Now.* New York: Charles Scribner's Sons, 1963.

———. *The Shaking of the Foundations.* New York: Charles Scribner's Sons, 1948.

Todorov, Tzvetan. *Facing the Extreme: Moral Life in the Concentration Camps.* Translated by Arthur Denner and Abigail Pollak. New York: Henry Holt, 1996.

———. *Hope and Memory: Lessons from the Twentieth Century.* Translated by David Bellos. Princeton: Princeton University Press, 2003.

Trilling, Lionel. *The Moral Obligation to Be Intelligent.* New York: Farrar, Straus and Giroux, 2000.

Twain, Mark. *The Works of Mark Twain: Early Tales & Sketches, Volume 1 1851–1864*. Edited by Edgar Marquess Branch and Robert H. Hirst. Berkeley: University of California Press, 1979.

Virgil. *The Aeneid.* Translated by Robert Fitzgerald. New York: Random House, 1983.

Weber, Max. *The Protestant Ethic and the Spirit of Capitalism.* Translated by Talcott Parsons. London: Routledge, 1992.

West, Cornel. *Race Matters.* New York: Vintage, 1994.

White, E. B. *Essays of E. B. White.* New York: Harper Perennial, 1992.

William of St. Thierry. *The Golden Epistle.* Translated by Theodore Berkeley. Kalamazoo, MI: Cistercian, 1980.

Wittgenstein, Ludwig. *Philosophical Grammar*. Edited by R. Rhees. Translated by Anthony Kenny. Oxford, UK: Blackwell, 1974. Quoted in *The Grammar of Faith,* by Paul Holmer, 185. San Francisco: Harper & Row, 1978.

Yeats, William Butler. "Meditations in Time of Civil War." In *The Collected Poems of W. B. Yeats.* Definitive edition. New York: Macmillan Publishing, 1956.

ACKNOWLEDGMENTS

I wrote this book at Princeton University while I was Lecturer in the Council of the Humanities and the Ferris Professor of Journalism. Carol Rigolot, David Kasunic, Cass Garner and Lin DeTitta made my time at Princeton productive and enjoyable. I will miss my office in the Joseph Henry House overlooking the quadrangle as well as my inquisitive and gifted students. The Ford Foundation provided generous and kind support. These two institutions, and the people who work there, made the book possible. I am very grateful.

The book was born out of a series of ten stories I wrote for *The New York Times,* although only six were incorporated into the book. Each story was based on one of the commandments. The stories ran consecutively in the paper. The stories would have never appeared, for there were some editors who did not see them as belonging in a newspaper, without the strong backing of Jon Landman, then the metropolitan editor, and Christine Kay, whose soaring talents as an editor are only outstripped by her kindness and compassion. I would also like to thank my colleagues at *Harper's,* especially Lewis H. Lapham and John R. MacArthur, as well as Robert Silvers at *The New York Review of Books* and Hamilton Fish, Taya Grobow, Janine Jaquet, Katrina vanden Heuvel, Jonathan Schell and Peggy Suttle at *The Nation.*

Pamela Diamond, who did the research and fact checking for the book, was as careful and meticulous as she was generous, thoughtful and patient. Her contributions were inestimable. Cabe Franklin also assisted with the research and helped organize the book. The Reverend Coleman Brown, the Reverend William Sloan Coffin, the Reverend Joe Hough, the Reverend Gordon Duggins, the Reverend Terry Burke and the Reverend Michael Granzen read the manuscript and gave me many ideas and suggestions, nearly all of which were incorporated. Coleman read the chapters as they were written, sending them back with long notes written in the margins or on yellow legal sheets. His wisdom brought several passages to his level, one that I and most all of his former students spend our lives trying to match. The Reverend William P. Mahedy, whose book *Out of the Night: The Spiritual Journey of Vietnam Vets* furthered my understanding of the journey back for combat veterans, kindly read through chapters as did Bishop George Packard, who was the subject of one of my chapters. Two great poets Gerald Stern and Larry Joseph also gave direction to the work. I was fortunate in the wisdom and help of Cynthia Adler, Stephen Arpadi, June Ballinger, Chris Bauman, David Callahan, Greg Carr, Kathy Coleman, John Henry Cox, Paul Golob, Michael Goldstein, Judy Herman, Sam Hynes, Michael Ignatieff, Stephen Kinzer, Norman Lear, Robert J. Lifton, Anne Marie Macari, Martin Marty, Terry Marx, Bill Moyers, Elaine Pagels, Kasey Pfaff, Ann and Walter Pincus, Samantha Power, Joe Sacco, Krister Stendahl, Richard Thomas, Serif Turgut, Judy Walgren, R. Foster Winans and Fred Wiseman. Barbara Moses, who could have been a great copy editor were she not a great painter, scoured the pages for errors before publication. And, of course, Kim Hedges, my favorite editor, read through draft after draft and saved me repeatedly from myself.

My colleagues at New York University were vital in helping administer the Ford Foundation grant and offering assistance.

They include Jay Rosen, Carol Sternhell, William and Judy Serrin, Michael and Beth Norman and Cathleen Dullahan. But most of all I want to thank Terence Culver, who worked with unstinting patience and effort to make the university's bureaucracy work, as did Jasodra Deowdhat.

There are no good writers without good editors. I have been fortunate in mine. Dominick Anfuso and Wylie O'Sullivan at Free Press formed and shaped the text. I am thankful for their energy, thoughtfulness and work. Lisa Bankoff of International Creative Management helped me handle the process of marketing and publishing the book and kept me on track and focused.

My mother, Teddy Hedges, as well as my uncle, Ellsworth Blair, have always given me unwavering encouragement. Finally, I must thank Thomas, Noëlle, Will and Annie. Writing is a solitary pursuit. I am fortunate in my interruptions.

INDEX

ABOUT THE AUTHOR

———◆———

CHRIS HEDGES was a foreign correspondent for nearly 20 years in Latin America, Africa, the Middle East and the Balkans. He worked for *The New York Times, The Dallas Morning News, The Christian Science Monitor* and National Public Radio. He holds a B.A. in English literature from Colgate University and a master of divinity from Harvard Divinity School. Hedges was a member of the *New York Times* team that won the 2002 Pulitzer Prize for Explanatory Reporting for the paper's coverage of global terrorism, and he received the 2002 Amnesty International Global Award for Human Rights Journalism. He has written for *Granta, Harper's, Foreign Affairs, Mother Jones, The Nation* and *The New York Review of Books.* He is the author of *War Is a Force That Gives Us Meaning,* which was a finalist for the National Book Critics Circle Award for Nonfiction, and *What Every Person Should Know About War.* A Senior Fellow at The Nation Institute, Hedges is also a Lecturer in the Council of the Humanities and teaches in the Program in American Studies at Princeton University. He lives near Princeton, New Jersey.